US Naval Air Power

West Coast 2010–20

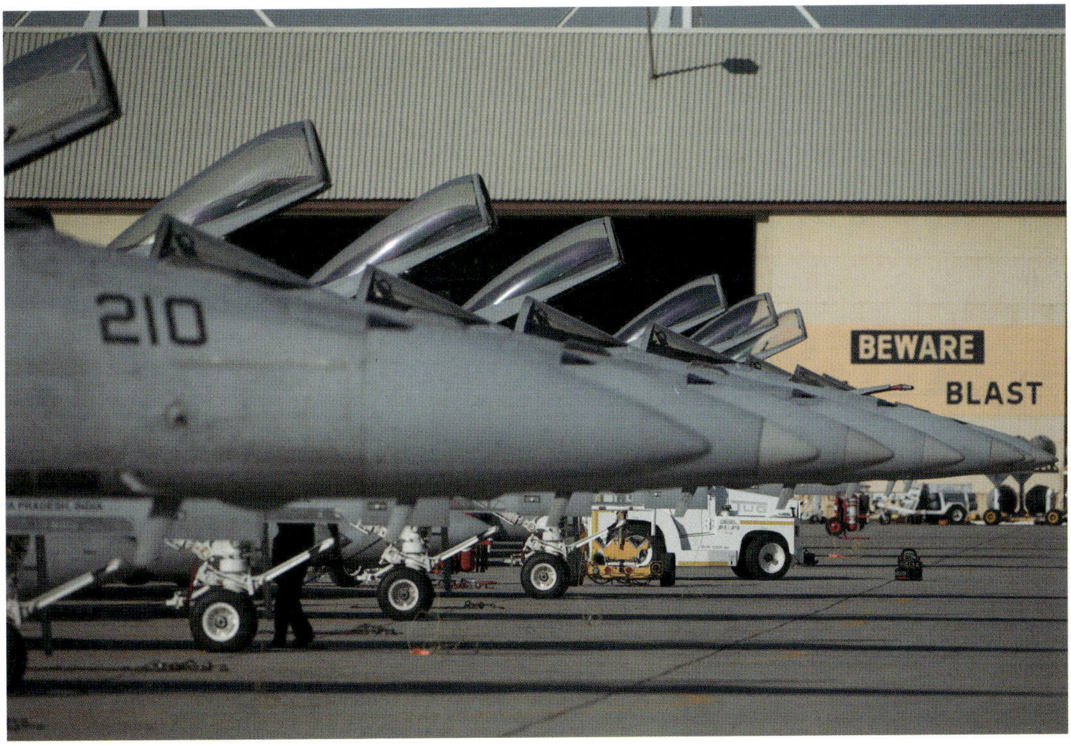

PATRICK ROEGIES

KEY Books

AIR FORCES SERIES, VOLUME 2

Front cover image: A VFA-2 "Bounty Hunter" F/A-18F, serial number 166811, performing a touch-and-go at the Lemoore runway during carrier deck landing practice.

Back cover image: Not a very common sight to see – all the aircraft of the squadron lined up on the flight line. In June 2017, VFA-2 "Bounty Hunters" just returned from its carrier deployment and "left" its aircraft on the NAS Lemoore platform before the aircraft were submitted to after-deployment inspections.

Title page image: The VFA-14 "Tophatters" flight line at NAS Lemoore in March 2014, preparing for the morning launch.

Contents page image: Four aircraft assigned to VFA-25 lined up on the taxi track, along with their "Red Air" adversaries for their next sortie during their carrier air wing training at NAS Fallon.

All images belong to the author.

Published by Key Books
An imprint of Key Publishing Ltd
PO Box 100
Stamford
Lincs PE19 1XQ

www.keypublishing.com

The right of Patrick Roegies to be identified as the author of this book has been asserted in accordance with the Copyright, Designs and Patents Act 1988 Sections 77 and 78.

Copyright © Patrick Roegies, 2021

ISBN 978 1 913870 24 9

All rights reserved. Reproduction in whole or in part in any form whatsoever or by any means is strictly prohibited without the prior permission of the Publisher.

Typeset by SJmagic DESIGN SERVICES, India.

Contents

Foreword 4

Chapter 1   Introduction 5

Chapter 2   100 Years of Naval Aviation 9

Chapter 3   Sequestration 2013 10

Chapter 4   Standardization 13

Chapter 5   Carrier Air Wing Developments 21

Chapter 6   West Coast Air Bases 37

Chapter 7   Naval Strike Fighter Developments 54

Chapter 8   Readiness Recovery Developments 63

Chapter 9   Naval Squadron Reforms 69

Chapter 10 Electronic Attack Squadron Developments 78

Chapter 11 Patrol Squadron Developments 81

Chapter 12 Carrier Airborne Early Warning Squadron Developments 84

Chapter 13 Training Squadron Developments 93

Chapter 14 Naval Air Warfare Development Center Developments 101

Chapter 15 Helicopter Sea Combat and Maritime Strike Squadron Developments 108

Chapter 16 Naval Test and Evaluation Developments 113

Chapter 17 Adversary Developments 116

Chapter 18 Remaining Developments 124

Chapter 19 Naval Aviation Modernization: The Future Air Wing 126

References 128

Foreword

The United States Naval Aviation celebrated its century of flight in 2011. Within its 100 years of existence, the Navy took a major leap in development from first to fifth generation and pushed the envelope of aviation technology. From the Curtiss biplane performing its first arrested landing and take-off from a Navy vessel to today's state-of-the-art fixed and rotary wing aircraft.

Naval Aviation is a story of vision, innovation, and continuous improvements. The past decade has presented many struggles in an ever-changing world, and the Navy command has managed to master all the challenges of keeping the service on top of the stage of naval air power.

Over the last ten years, the Navy invested significant time and effort to standardize the fleet of both fixed and rotary wing aircraft within its operational inventory, while carefully introducing and implementing stealth technology within its capabilities.

The US Navy undertook all required efforts with a strong vision to continue delivering combat readiness; this included integration of new aircraft types, development of subtypes (including integration of technological, state-of-the-art systems in existing aircraft types). Furthermore, the Navy coped with the challenges of maintaining the existing fleet to combat readiness status, standardization programs, and several Service Life Extension Programs.

This book describes the Naval Air Power developments on the West Coast between 2010 and 2020. These developments influenced all aspects within the service and included the challenges that were met and resolved, the developments taking place within this past decade, and the developments in Naval Air Station (NAS), Carrier Air Wing (CVW), and squadron rotations.

The document written by the US Marine Corps, *Naval Aviation Vision 2016–2025*, defines two major fields of focus for the United States Naval Aviation departments going forward. The first is defined as the strategic imperative of expanding capabilities through technological advancement, in order to deliver integrated warfighting capabilities (defined as "the combined interaction of people, equipment and training to launch weapons or gather intelligence").

The second is defined as maintaining capacity. Capacity includes: (1) the ideas of aggregate capacity, which is the "total number of units manned, trained and equipped to meet steady-state presence and crisis-response requirements"; (2) operational capacity, which is the number and readiness of "aircraft within a squadron and the number of aircrews available to operate them" in order to succeed in combat. The latter refers more specifically to the Naval Aviation department, and the "Vision" document includes a roadmap on how to maintain the desired key performance indicator of 85 percent combat readiness for aviation assets.

A special courtesy to the public affairs officers Theresa McKenrick, Melinda Larson, Lydia Bock, Zip Upham, Kristopher Haugh, and Vance Vasquez of the West Coast bases, enabling many visits, hosting interviews, and allowing the gathering of photographic material. Also, a special courtesy for LT Matthew "Abe" Gottschalk, public affairs officer of VFC-13, LT Glenn Diller, public affairs officer of VFA-97, LT Alex Bowman, public affairs officer at VFA-41, CDR Colin "Doris" Day, and CDR Jason "Chubbs" Fox of Airborne Command and Control and Logistics Wing for assisting in the composition of this book.

Lastly, a word of gratitude for the people who supported me during the compilation of this book, starting with my wife, Joyce Roegies Vlieks, and my fellow aviation passionists, Jurgen van Toor, Marco Dijkshoorn, Paul Gross, Hans Antonissen, Theo van Vliet, Ben Gorski, and Twan van Dommelen; all have checked the contents of this book and accompanied me on many trips to the United States for visits to the various Naval air stations.

Chapter 1
Introduction

In 2011, US Naval Aviation celebrated its 100th Anniversary. From its formation in 1911 until today, the US Naval Air Force has increased to an extensive size and is used as an effective force to rapidly deploy to conflicts throughout the world. Forward presence, deterrence, sea control, power projection, maritime security, and humanitarian assistance are the six missions currently specified for the maritime strategy. Today's Naval Aviation comprises more than 100,000 officers and sailors assigned to 11 aircraft carriers, nine carrier air wings, 25 Naval Air Stations, and 168 fleet, reserve, and training squadrons. Another three aircraft carriers are currently under construction: CVN-79 USS *John F. Kennedy* is planned for commissioning in 2022, CVN-80 USS *Enterprise* is planned for commissioning in 2029, and CVN-81 USS *Doris Miller* is planned for commissioning in 2032 and will possibly replace the aging Nimitz class carriers.

With the standardization to the Hornet platform starting in the 1980s and 1990s, the Navy prepared for an effective and efficient use of its assets all over the world. The introduction of the Super Hornet in 1999 continued this movement with further standardization. Although currently the US Navy (USN) still operates a number of Legacy Hornets at the Naval Air Warfare Development Center (NAWDC), and several Naval Adversary Squadrons, all remaining Strike Fighter Squadrons have completed their conversion to the Super Hornet the past decade. In August 2017, the Navy stated their intent to complete the conversion of the remaining Legacy Hornet squadrons. VFA-37 "Bulls" and VFA-131 "Wildcats" converted to the Super Hornet in 2017 and early 2018, respectively. VFA-34 "Blue Blasters" was the very last operational squadron operating the Legacy Hornet, completing the conversion to the F/A-18E by February 1, 2019.

With the final conversion of NAS Lemoore-based VFA-113 "Stingers" and VFA-94 "Mighty Shrikes" to the F/A-18E/F Super Hornet, the major West Coast strike fighter base had completed its conversion to this fourth-generation carrier-capable fighter aircraft. In order to balance the capabilities between the East Coast- and the West Coast-based carrier air wings, VFA-86 "Sidewinders" was relocated from MCAS Beaufort to NAS Lemoore in 2011 and became part of Carrier Air Wing 2. During the summer of 2016, VFA-136 "Knighthawks" was relocated from NAS Oceana to NAS Lemoore and became part of Carrier Air Wing 1.

Furthermore, all the Electronic Attack Squadrons or VAQ squadrons have completed their conversion to the EA-18G Growler. The EA-18G Growlers replaced the aging EA-6B Prowlers based at NAS Whidbey Island. The EA-6B had been a venerable platform for the Navy for many years. However, the Navy needed a replacement, as the service life and end of life age for the Prowlers was reached. That replacement ended up being the EA-18G Growler, as an evolution of the reliable Hornet platform. This conversion was completed as well, with VAQ-129 exchanging its Prowlers for Growlers in 2013, leaving VAQ-131 "Lancers" and VAQ-134 as the last remaining Prowler squadrons within the Navy. VAQ-131 was scheduled for the final deployment operating the EA-6B Prowler in January 2014 but were instead rescheduled to start its transition to the EA-18G Growler earlier than anticipated. After training in its new jet with the VAQ Fleet Replacement Squadron (FRS), VAQ-129, the squadron was awarded safe for flight status on April 23, 2015. The final squadron, VAQ-134 "Garudas," transitioned to the EA-18G Growler in 2016 and was the last squadron to complete the conversion.

NAS Whidbey Island remains the main EA-18G Growler base, with deliveries continuing in 2020. VAQ-144 will be formed at NAS Whidbey Island on October 1, 2021, equipped with the EA-18G

Growler. Full operational capability will be achieved in Fiscal Year (FY) 2023 to meet scheduled operational requirements for the squadron. VAQ-144 will report to Commander, Electronic Attack Wing Pacific (COMVAQWINGPAC) as part of the Commander, Naval Air Force, United States Pacific Fleet (COMNAVAIRPAC).

The F-35C also made its first appearance within the operational Strike Fighter Squadrons. With the Initial Operational Capability (IOC) milestone set between August 2018 and February 2019, the first F-35C Lightning IIs arrived at the FRS, also referred to as Replacement Air Group (RAG) squadrons. East Coast squadron, VFA-101 "Grim Reapers," was the initial Naval squadron to receive the F-35C in May 2012, and VMFA-501 was the first Marine Corps squadron to receive the F-35B Vertical Take-Off and Landing (VTOL) aircraft. VMFA-501 "Warlords," based at MCAS Beaufort, currently operate as the F-35B FRS. The squadron has assumed the lineage of VMFA-451 "Blue Devils," which was decommissioned on January 31, 1997.

VFA-125 "Rough Raiders" FRS at NAS Lemoore was the initial West Coast squadron to receive the F-35C. The squadron was originally formed on November 13, 1980, at NAS Lemoore. The squadron was the Navy's first F/A-18 squadron to receive the factory fresh F/A-18A and F/A-18B aircraft. VFA-125 received its first aircraft in April 1981 and, by March 1985, had completed over 30,000 mishap-free flight hours in the Hornet. On October 1, 2010, VFA-125 was decommissioned as an F/A-18 FRS, and its aircraft and personnel were transferred and integrated within VFA-122 "Flying Eagles." On January 12, 2017, VFA-125 was reactivated and is the West Coast F-35C FRS once again. It is the FRS for the latest fifth-generation fighter, also adopting the aircraft from VFA-101 Strike Fighter Squadron. VFA-101 had just two F-35C Joint Strike Fighter jets remaining on May 23, 2019, when the squadron deactivated.

This fifth-generation fighter possesses stealth capabilities and state-of-the-art electronic systems, avionics, and communication systems. This allows the F-35 to communicate with multiple other platforms. Current plans include the purchase of a total of 260 F-35C aircraft by the US Navy and an additional 80 F-35B aircraft by the US Marines Corps. Since the 260 aircraft will not make up for the replacement of all the F/A-18s, the Hornet squadrons will supplement the F-35 squadrons in the future. Thus, the F-35C will be operating alongside the F/A-18 Hornet for at least the next decade.

Besides the F-35C program, there are several other upgrades within the carrier air wings in development, modernizing, and replacing the aging components within the air wings. As of 2020, the P-3 Orion has almost entirely been replaced by the P-8 Poseidon. The E-2D has made its appearance within the operational Carrier Airborne Early Warning Squadrons, also referred to as VAW squadrons. Also, the C-2A Greyhound aircraft are in the process of being replaced. This transition from the C-2A to CMV-22B is expected to span from 2020 to 2026. The H-60 Sea Hawk remains the main standardized helicopter platform within the air wings, with continuous improvement projects running.

In 2016, Carrier Air Wing 2 was reassigned to USS *Carl Vinson*. The wing's next deployment was to the Western Pacific, January 23–June 23, 2017. Shortly after their arrival, the aircraft of VFA-2 "Bounty Hunters" were parked at the NAS Lemoore flight line, awaiting some heavily necessary tender loving care.

Finally, the unmanned RQ-4 Global Hawk program is currently underway. These are the focus of the Naval Aviation modernization programs over the next decade.

Another current modernization program is the upgrade of the Airborne Early Warning (AEW) E-2C Hawkeye to E-2D standard. The E-2C has been the carrier-based aircraft for the Navy for more than 30 years. The modernizations to the E-2C commenced in FY2003. This program was carried out by Raytheon, Northrop Grumman, and Lockheed Martin. The modernization program comprised an improved state-of-the-art radar suite, a new Total Radiation Aperture Control Antenna (TRAC-A) system including upgraded avionics, systems, and communication system integrated. These enable the E-2 to perform significantly heavier jamming. The radar and automated data processing system can handle more than 600 tracks. An Identification Friend or Foe system (IFF) was also integrated in the upgrade of the aircraft.

The E-2 was originally equipped with the AP-120 and AP-125 radar and has been upgraded in the past decades to the APS-138 and APS-139 standard. With the improved APS-145(V) radar, the operating range of the E-2 significantly increased as well. The operating range increased by 40 percent, and the surveillance space volume increased by 96 percent, being able to scan more than 2,000 tracks simultaneously.

Further ongoing developments led to the Lot 5 E-2D "Advanced Hawkeye" program. In the E-2D, an advanced radar, data communication, drone control capabilities, and a cruise missile launch intercept system were integrated. This makes the E-2D the first aircraft able to detect an air-to-ground missile launch.

The new AN/APY-9 radar is a combined ultra-high frequency (UHF) mechanical and electronically scanned radar system, with the ability to counter stealth technology. The improved radar system also provides an improved AEW situational awareness capability within the area of operations. The radar can operate in three separate modes: Advanced Airborne Early Warning Surveillance mode, Enhanced Sector Scan mode, and Enhanced Tracking Sector mode.

With the integration of the drone, the control system of the E-2D can also upload images, video, and surveillance material obtained by drones, and enables the crew of the E-2D to analyze intelligence, surveillance, and reconnaissance (ISR) target data in real time to prevent a secondary launch.

Operating alongside the F/A-18 and EA-18G Growler, the E-2D is an integral part of the Naval Integrated Fire Control-Counter Air (NIFC-CA), a program designed to integrate early warning, surveillance, and weapons control systems to protect the friendly forces in the area of operations.

The latest developments of the E-2D program include the possibility for in-flight air refueling. With this aerial refueling capability, the all-weather, carrier-based, tactical battle management AEW, and command and control aircraft will be able to remain airborne to the limits of the aircrew and airframe endurance. As a result, a carrier air wing will now deploy five Advanced Hawkeye aircraft during a cruise instead of four, as was previously standard.

The modernization on the first five aircraft was conducted at Northrop Grumman in FY2015, followed by another five in FY2016. For FY2017, an additional six aircraft were planned. After FY2017, an additional 23 aircraft were planned to be purchased. The first squadron to receive the modernized E-2D aircraft was VAW-125, based at NAS Norfolk on the East Coast. This unit is now forward deployed to NAS Iwakuni.

VFA-147 performed its conversion training with VFA-125 using its aircraft. When the squadron received its factory fresh F-35C Lightning II aircraft, the squadron also received brand-new facilities, including a new hangar and sunsheds on its flight line positioned directly next to VFA-125 "Rough Raiders" facilities.

On May 14, 2020, the US Navy announced the final P-3C Orion MPA Squadron completed its transition to the P-8A Poseidon. The final active-duty Airborne Patrol Squadron, VP-40 "Fighting Marlins," completed its transition from the Lockheed P-3C Orion to the Boeing P-8A Poseidon maritime patrol aircraft.

VP-40 began the conversion to the P-8A platform in November 2019, following its return to NAS Whidbey Island, after completing its final active-duty P-3C deployment. The conclusion of the forward deployment of VP-40 ended 52 years of P-3 Orion operations, which began in 1968.

The squadron transferred the last of its nine P-3C aircraft, with the delivery of bureau number (BuNo) 162776 to the Naval Aviation Museum in Pensacola, Florida. The squadron commenced P-8A transition training under the instruction of VP-30, which fulfills the Patrol and Reconnaissance FRS duties, based out of NAS Jacksonville. VP-30 has been conducting squadron transitions to the P-8A since 2012, utilizing a team of military and civilian maintenance and aircrew professionals. The main West Coast Patrol Squadron base is NAS Whidbey Island, comprising six P-8A Poseidon squadrons in 2020.

Over the past decade, the Navy also took a significant effort to standardize its rotary capacity to the MH-60S Knighthawk and MH-60R Seahawk. Starting in 1997, the Navy decided to replace its venerable CH-46 Sea Knight helicopters. After sea demonstrations by a converted UH-60, the Navy awarded a production contract to Sikorsky for the CH-60S in 1998.

The multi-mission Sikorsky MH-60S Knighthawk helicopter entered service in February 2002. The US Navy used the MH-60S helicopters to carry out missions such as vertical replenishment, combat search and rescue, special warfare support, and airborne mine countermeasures.

Sikorsky Aircraft developed the MH-60R Seahawk multi-mission naval helicopter, also referred to as "Romeo," in order to replace the legacy SH-60B and SH-60F helicopter fleet. The MH-60R integrated advanced mission systems and sensors developed by Lockheed Martin Mission Systems and Training (MST). The helicopter was intended to carry out a range of missions, including anti-submarine warfare (ASW), anti-surface warfare (ASuW), surveillance, communications relay, search and rescue (SAR), naval gunfire support (NGFS), personnel transport, vertical replenishment (VERTREP), and logistics support. Both the MH-60S and MH-60R helicopters can be launched from aircraft carriers, destroyers, cruise ships, frigates, and amphibious ships. On the West Coast, NAS North Island currently hosts fifteen helicopter squadrons.

Besides the development within the Helicopter Maritime Strike (HSM) and the Sea Combat Helicopter squadrons, the Navy also started the definition phase of its helicopter training capabilities, now fulfilled by the TH-57B/C helicopter. The TH-57B/C is commercially referred to as a Bell 206B-3 and was purchased by the Navy in 1989. On January 14, 2020, the Navy announced it selected the Leonardo TH-119 for its future helicopter trainer fleet. The decision analysis included three alternatives, which also included the Bell Helicopter-designed light, single-engined 407GXi Helicopter and the Airbus Helicopter light, twin-engined H135.

An initial contract comprised the delivery of the first 32 TH-119 helicopters, which were designated by the Navy as the TH-73A. The total contract comprised the procurement of 130 aircraft. Deliveries were scheduled to begin in calendar year 2020 and continue through calendar year 2024. On November 14, 2020, the Navy announced the acquisition of 36 additional TH-73A helicopters. These helicopters will mainly be based on the East Coast at NAS Whiting Field-South.

A detail shot of two VFC-13 "Saints" F-5N Tiger IIs at the Fallon Runway just seconds before take-off.

Chapter 2
100 Years of Naval Aviation

In 2011, several aircraft received a commemorate camouflage painting, and several airshows were hosted to honor the 100 years of Naval Aviation. However, at the time, the Navy was operating within a tight national fiscal environment, with the Department of Defense (DoD) undergoing extreme cutbacks. These cutbacks would significantly influence the Naval air power capabilities during the next decade while still supporting the US Naval strategy. This strategy involved pursuing the following missions: Forward Presence, Deterrence, Sea Control, Power Projection, Maritime Security, and Humanitarian Assistance and Disaster Response.

The Navy strategy would continue to adapt to the challenges of a changing world environment, to operate jointly with partners at sea, on land, and in the air. As an indispensable partner to Naval Aviation, the Navy developed new platforms, sensors, and weapons systems to meet future threats during peace and wartime. The emphasis would, however, be placed on reducing costs and development time while leveraging technological advantages to increase automation and further decrease manpower requirements. This effort would be relevant in areas such as maintenance by standardization, fueling, arming, and logistics.

Naval Aviation looked to a future "Navy after next," where aircraft carriers and air wings were well-equipped with state-of-the-art technology to deter and defeat future threats. From 2011 until 2031, new aircraft in many Navy mission areas would commence development to replace their aging counterparts and provide the bridge toward the future. The future, however, would be built on the present and the past. Above all else, Naval Aviation would continue to fly, fight, and win.

Above left: VFA-147 was selected to be the first operational squadron to transition to the F-35C in January 2018. During the transition period the squadron was still assigned to Carrier Air Wing 11.

Above right: During start-up, a number of checks are performed prior to commencing the taxi-run to the runway. The groundcrew assists the start-up while communicating with the pilot.

Chapter 3
Sequestration 2013

The Navy faced some very challenging times early in the 2010s. A sequestration presented itself and required sacrifices from all services. As a result of the sequestration of late 2013, four carrier air wings were to be grounded and eight carrier deployments were canceled, including two that were already underway. These actions helped save billions of dollars and the Navy Secretary stated these drastic actions would not damage the presence of the Navy overseas.

However, these cuts were felt almost immediately in the carrier air wings. With the immediate grounding of four carrier air wings, the Navy Aviation readiness capacity would be directly affected and drastically reduced; four of the nine CVWs were grounded and two more operating at minimum safe flying levels. Top Navy officials warned that it would take the better part of the year, and up to three times the cost, to return these air wings to full readiness. The four nominated CVWs were Carrier Air Wing 2, with the Abraham Lincoln Carrier Strike Group (CSG); Carrier Air Wing 9, with John C. Stennis CSG; Carrier Air Wing 17, with Carl Vinson CSG; and Carrier Air Wing 7, with Dwight Eisenhower CSG. In addition, the two air wings dropping to a "tactical hard deck" were Carrier Air Wing 1, with the Theodore Roosevelt CSG, and Carrier Air Wing 11, with Nimitz CSG. Basic flight training for pilot and flight officer trainees would halt in March 2014.

Thankfully, Naval Aviation forces were able to minimize the effects of the 2013 sequestration and continue to meet their operational and forward presence commitments. The shutdown of carrier air wings was avoided, with only two reduced to minimum flight hours. The training of all aircrews was sustained, and simulator use was maximized. However, a substantial number of aircraft and engine procurement and overhauls were affected by budget cuts.

The Chief of Naval Operations (CNO) warned about the potential effects of a continued sequestration in 2014, speculating that the Naval Aviation forces would lose approximately 25 aircraft in procurement and, besides the 90 aircraft overhauls that were canceled in 2013, another 190 heavily overdue aircraft overhauls would have to be canceled at the Fleet Readiness Centers during 2014.

With the sequestration cuts to federal budgets having gone into effect on March 1, 2014, the Navy Secretary announced on March 2, 2014, a series of alternatives that included reduced operations for carrier air wings and renegotiation of procurement contracts. Initially, it was announced that the Navy would "shut down" Carrier Air Wing 2 in April and initiate the preparations to gradually stand down

As a result of a severe shortage of spare parts, the combat readiness of the Super Hornet fleet did not meet its key performance indicators. Aircraft were parked in short-term storage until spare parts became available again. Seen here is BuNo 165886 at the NAS Lemoore flight line awaiting spare parts.

flying in at least three additional carrier air wings, with two more CVWs being reduced to minimum safe flying levels by the end of the year. When the final resolution passed in March, these cuts were limited in terms of sequestration and the need to shut down the CVWs was prevented.

The Commander Naval Air Forces, or "Air Boss," fought for tactical hard deck funding, meaning funding the minimum amount of flight hours needed to keep an aviator current in type, typically 11 hours of flight time per aviator per month for most aircraft types, as cited in a 2009 study by the Center for Naval Analyses. This report concluded that funding 11 flight hours per month met baseline flight proficiency for safety.

As a result, the Navy initially managed to keep its ten carrier air wings operational, with two CVWs, or 16 squadrons, reduced to the tactical hard deck level and held to a baseline proficiency as opposed to a shutdown. It is easier to recover from tactical hard deck, and at significantly less cost, than if they were to shut down, and FY2013 provided enough room to maneuver for the Naval Air Forces to realize that. The squadrons in the two affected CVWs were in a recovery phase at the end of FY2013, after a 90-day tactical hard deck period. The non-carrier squadrons, such as patrol squadrons, were less affected by the sequestration, having a tighter timeline for how they rotate for workups and deployment. Most were already positioned during the latter half of the fiscal year, but managing their funding was a difficult task, nonetheless.

As the Naval Air Forces flew almost a half million hours, the squadrons proceeded in a fashion that kept the Navy at readiness levels of fully deployed and at full strength, for the most part, the ashore-based squadrons were without any significant handicap. Historically, the Navy annually experiences a shortage of flight hours as the end of a fiscal year approaches but, in 2013, the service managed to avoid this scenario, even with the burden of sequestration.

The Navy was also able to sustain the carrier qualifications for student aviators and aviators in type training with fleet readiness squadrons in 2013. Simulators were used to train aircrews due to the sequestration's limit on flight hours, especially with the squadrons in tactical hard deck mode.

Under the Naval Aviation Simulation Master Plan, set in motion in 2012, the Navy was pushing toward maximum use of simulators inside its training and readiness matrix to reduce flight hours required for training. The service is in the process of upgrading and increasing the number of simulators to reach this future goal.

Short-term Planning

After the sequestration, follow-up studies commenced at NAS Lemoore, with an intended completion date in the spring of 2014. These studies included the arrival and successful integration of the F-35C on the West Coast between 2015 and 2016. The Navy was developing a variant of the stealth F-35 joint strike fighter as its next-generation carrier-based tactical aircraft. The aircraft would replace the F/A-18 Legacy Hornet and complement the newer Super Hornet in projecting sea-based air power around the globe.

In addition to being much more survivable than the Super Hornet, due to its integrated stealth design, the carrier variant of the F-35 would have a 60 percent greater unrefueled combat radius in air-to-air missions and a 40 percent greater radius in air-to-ground bombing missions, carrying similar payloads of munitions. The study comprised two alternatives in which 100 aircraft would be based either at NAF El Centro or at NAS Lemoore. If NAS Lemoore was selected as a future home base, the new F-35C would replace the current aircraft on a one-to-one basis and if NAF El Centro was selected, the airfield would gain 100 aircraft.

Long-term Planning

The development of the F-35C intended to transform carrier-based air operations in the future. The first Navy squadrons have converted to the F-35 already. VFA-101 "Grim Reapers," which was the last squadron to operate the trusted F-14 aircraft, was relocated to Eglin Air Force Base (AFB) to get familiar with the tactics of the aircraft in order to train future F-35C pilots and pilot instructors. On May 23, 2019, VFA-101 "Grim Reapers" was deactivated, and its aircraft were adopted into the remaining F-35C FRS, VFA-125 "Rough Raiders" and relocated to NAS Lemoore.

Besides the Navy, the Marines also started at Eglin AFB with conversion squadron VMFAT-501 "Warlords" in order to prepare and train pilots and pilot instructors for the Vertical Short Take Off and Landing (VSTOL) version of the F-35. VMFAT-501 relocated to MCAS Beaufort in July 2014, as a part of MAG-31.

In addition, the first Marines squadron, VMFA-121 "Green Knights" — based at MCAS Yuma at that time — had already transferred to the F-35B and became operational on September 28, 2012. This was the primary squadron to be equipped with the F-35. The Navy has two operational F-35C squadrons, VFA-147 "Argonauts" and VFA-97 "Warhawks," with VFA-25 "Fist of the Fleet" being the next selected squadron to make the conversion.

Given the advantages of the aircraft, like low observable characteristics and increased situational awareness for the pilot, this could allow strike fighters to use just four aircraft on missions instead of 12. This would mean a reduction in assets of approximately 60 percent. However, with an above average number of alternatives, the Navy has sent confusing signals about its vision toward the future program, which might result in a possible delay in funding. Any such delay could impair the plans of other services to acquire their F-35 aircraft and would inevitably raise questions about the future utility of carrier-based air power.

It is possible that none of these speculations about impending cuts to Navy programs will come true. For instance, any bid by the Navy to delay fielding its version of the F-35 would run head-on into assurances by senior Pentagon policymakers that they intend to protect the joint program from budget cuts. However, while the F-35 may be safe, it is clear that many other programs will have to be delayed, abandoned, or canceled to bring military plans into alignment with spending caps imposed by budget law. Sequestration, originally envisioned as a way of putting federal finances on a more sustainable footing, is rapidly becoming the biggest threat to US military power.

VFA-147 completed the conversion to the F-35C in October 2018, when assigned to Carrier Air Wing 11. The squadron was then transferred to Carrier Air Wing 2, preparing for the first F-35 deployment on board the CVN-70 USS *Carl Vinson*.

Just prior to the conversion to the F-35C, VFA-97 "Warhawks" fulfilled a temporary adversary role. The originally received batch of FY2012, Lot 36 Hornets were traded in to be transferred to the remaining operational Strike Fighter Squadrons and the squadron received older models from VFA-137 "Kestrels" and VFA-192 "Golden Dragons."

Chapter 4
Standardization

In the last decade, US Naval Aviation forces have put tremendous efforts into the standardization of its fighter and attack assets, reducing the number of different aircraft types and integrating their tasks into the F/A-18 Hornet platform. The Legacy Hornets, referring to the F/A-18A–D versions, created new opportunities for the USN. The aircraft is capable of performing all the fighter and ground attack missions appointed to the carrier air wings. With the arrival of the EA-18G Growler, the electronic warfare component, the latest version of the Hornet was integrated. In the early 2000s, the aging F/A-18A and B Legacy models were mostly transferred to the Marines, and the F/A-18C and D models were replaced by the F/A-18E and F Super Hornets by 2010. Initially, a total of 257 Super Hornets were ordered during FY2005–09, which were delivered between 2007 and 2012 under a multi-year procurement program awarded to Boeing on December 29, 2003. While deliveries were still underway, multi-year procurement program II (MYP II) included an additional 210 F/A-18E, F/A-18F, and EA-18G aircraft ordered from FY2009 onwards. The initial MYP II was expanded with an additional 47 aircraft, of which 24 were to be delivered to the Australian Air Force. MYP III was signed on September 28, 2010 and included the delivery of 66 F/A-18E and F/A-18F aircraft and 58 EA-18G aircraft to be delivered from 2013 onwards.

A total of more than 604 Super Hornets and Growlers have been delivered to the Navy, as of April 2020. In 2019, Boeing received a US$4bn contract to deliver 78 additional Block III Super Hornets for the Navy through FY2021. The Navy plans to sign year-to-year contracts with Boeing to convert all its Block II aircraft to Block III variants until 2033. With this plan in place, the carrier air wings can perform virtually every mission in the appointed tactical mission spectrum, which includes air superiority, fighter escort, close air support, precision guided weapons, day and night strike capabilities, suppression of hostile air defenses, reconnaissance, tanker missions, and electronic warfare.

Lot 12 F/A-18C-30-MC Hornet BuNo 164027 was first noted as modex 36 in September 2019 at NAS Fallon. This aircraft was previously assigned to VFA-125, modex NJ-311, where it started its operational career. The F/A-18C was also assigned to VFA-147, VFA-97, VFA-94, and VFA-22 before it was transferred to NAWDC. The NAWDC aircraft that have reached their maximum hours are traded out with other Legacy Hornets, which were replaced by the Super Hornet or the F-35C Lightning II.

Further Integrating the Super Hornet

By 2010, the Navy operated seven different types of Hornets. Although the older A and B models were not serving with the operational squadrons, they still resided within test squadrons; Naval Strike and Air Warfare Center (NSAWC), later renamed to NAWDC; Adversary Reserve Squadrons; and the FRSs. The last remaining F/A-18C and D models were scheduled to be replaced by the end of 2015. By February 4, 2019, the last Legacy Hornet left the operational Strike Fighter Squadrons. Test and Evaluation Squadron VX-9 "Dust Devils" also withdrew its last Legacy Hornet from use on September 22, 2020, leaving only a handful of Legacy Hornets with NAWDC.

The F/A-18C and D models were passed on to the Marines squadrons to replace their older A and B models. At Marines Corps Air Station (MCAS) Miramar, the conversion to the C and D models had been completed, with most of the A and B models that were replaced transferred to the Aerospace Maintenance and Regeneration Group (AMARG) aircraft storage facility, located at Davis-Monthan AFB in Tucson, Arizona.

As of 2012, the mid-term plan included the relocation of two East Coast squadrons to the West Coast. This relocation was deemed necessary in order to provide enough Strike Fighter Squadrons to meet the changing operational demand in the Pacific. It also enabled the Navy to mitigate a possible shortage in the Strike Fighter community assets, due to the aging F/A-18 Legacy Hornet aircraft. Conversion of up to an additional five Strike Fighter Squadrons from Legacy Hornet to Super Hornet squadrons resulted in the alignment of assets to meet carrier air wing deployment schedules, and to ensure sufficient Strike Fighter capability was present in the short term.

Another reason for the relocation of two East Coast Super Hornet squadrons was to geographically align and equally divide the Strike Fighter Squadrons with the current carrier air wing deployment requirements. At the time, two East Coast squadrons were the subject of multiple cross-continental transits to train and certify with the aircraft carrier and carrier strike group. Relocating the East Coast Strike Fighter Squadrons to NAS Lemoore provided necessary support without duplication of existing home-base support functions and realigned the fleet with East/West operational commitments.

The two squadrons nominated to be relocated to NAS Lemoore were VFA-11 "Red Rippers" and VFA-136 "Knighthawks." Eventually, VFA-11 "Red Rippers" remained at NAS Oceana. Specifically, the proposed Strike Fighter realignment consisted of the following primary actions:

VFA-113 "Stingers" was one of the last squadrons to make the conversion to the F/A-18E. On February 17, 2016, the final F/A-18C departed the VFA-113 flight line and was transferred to NAS Oceana, Virginia.

- VFA-136 "Knighthawks" arrived at NAS Lemoore in 2014 as a ten-aircraft F/A-18E squadron;
- Three existing squadrons transitioned from a ten-aircraft Legacy Hornet squadrons to a ten-aircraft Super Hornet squadron, starting in 2013;
- One existing squadron transitioned from a ten-aircraft Legacy Hornet squadron to a ten-aircraft Super Hornet squadron in 2014;
- One existing squadron transitioned from a ten-aircraft Legacy Hornet squadron to a 12-aircraft Super Hornet squadron in 2015;
- As a separate action, NAS Lemoore aimed to reduce the number of training aircraft in its training squadron, VFA-122, between 2012 and 2013;
- Hangars 1, 2, and 4 were to be modified for the purpose of hosting the Super Hornets.

In July 2011, VFA-86 "Sidewinders" left MCAS Beaufort and moved to NAS Lemoore, transitioning to the F/A-18E Super Hornet. Eventually, in the summer of 2016, VFA-136 "Knighthawks," assigned to CVW-1, which was assigned to CVN-75 USS *Harry S. Truman*, moved from NAS Oceana to NAS Lemoore. VFA-11 "Red Rippers" remained at NAS Oceana.

By 2014, the conversion from F/A-18 squadrons to Super Hornet squadrons was in full progress at NAS Lemoore. The squadrons VFA-97 "Warhawks" and VFA-192 "Golden Dragons" were part of the conversion process, with VFA-97's conversion to Super Hornets commencing in December 2013. The last "Warhawks" Legacy Hornets left NAS Lemoore in November 2013, and the first Super Hornets arrived at the squadron on December 2, 2013. VFA-97 took delivery of a brand-new factory delivered F/A-18E Super Hornets carrier. Deck qualifications took place in February 2014 on the USS *George Bush* and were completed successfully.

VFA-192 "Golden Dragons" received its first Super Hornets in January 2014 but, in contrast to VFA-97, it did not receive factory new F/A-18Es. The "Golden Dragons" received used airframes from other squadrons. Each aircraft received was subjected to thorough maintenance, in practice meaning that the entire airframe was stripped and inspected.

NAS Lemoore operates a search and rescue squadron equipped with four MH-60S Seahawk helicopters. The squadron is nicknamed "Wranglers." BuNo 165755, seen here, received modex 7S-01.

By 2014, the remaining squadrons at NAS Lemoore operating the Legacy Hornets were VFA-94, VFA-113, and VFA-146.

After returning from its April–December 2013 deployment with CVW-11 aboard CVN-68 USS *Nimitz*, VFA-146 "Blue Diamonds" underwent an extensive maintenance phase to transfer 14 Lot 10 F/A-18C Legacy Hornets to other squadrons and AMARG. From December 2014 to May 2015, the "Blue Diamonds" transitioned from Lot 10 Hornets to Lot 24 F/A-18 Super Hornets. On May 26, 2015, the "Blue Diamonds" achieved their Safe-for-Flight in the Super Hornet.

Shortly after returning from its August 2014–June 2015 deployment with CVW-17 aboard CVN-70 USS *Carl Vinson*, VFA-94 "Mighty Shrikes" flew its last sortie in the F/A-18C Hornet on August 26, 2015. Soon after, the squadron began its conversion to the two-seat F/A-18F Super Hornet and began to receive its Lot 25 F/A-18F Super Hornets. After a six-month transition syllabus, the "Mighty Shrikes" were declared Safe-For-Flight in the Super Hornet in March 2016.

Starting in late 2015, VFA-113 transitioned aircraft and acquired a brand-new set of 12 F/A-18E Super Hornets. These were, at the time, some of the newest and most capable Rhinos in the fleet. On February 17, 2016, the final F/A-18C departed the VFA-113 flight line and was transferred to NAS Oceana, Virginia. As the last Navy F/A-18C squadron on the West Coast to transition to the Super Hornet, that last flight happened to be the last operational Legacy Hornet flight ever for NAS Lemoore.

In 2017, the markings on the aircraft were toned down. The current squadron markings are more visibly presented on the tail section.

After its return from a deployment with Carrier Air Wing 11 on the CVN-68 USS *Nimitz* from January 24, 2008 until June 3, 2008, VFA-41 began trading in its originally received Lot 26 F/A-18F Hornets for Lot 30 F/A-18F Hornets which were fitted with AESA radar technology.

Standardization

Groundcrew preparing for a next sortie at the NAS Lemoore flight line.

VFA-86 "Sidewinders" is a long-term operator of the F/A-18 Hornet. On July 15, 1987, VA-86 was officially redesignated VFA-86, and began operating the F/A-18C Hornet. It was the first East Coast squadron to receive the first Lot 10 F/A-18C models.

There have been two distinct Navy squadrons known as the "Flying Eagles." The first was established in 1950 as VC-35, later redesignated VA(AW)-35, and then VA-122 and was disestablished in May 1991. Often, the new squadron will assume the nickname, insignia, and traditions of the earlier squadrons. However, officially, the US Navy does not recognize a direct lineage with decommissioned squadrons if a new squadron is formed with the same designation. In January 1999, a new "Flying Eagles" squadron was established as VFA-122, the first squadron to operate the F/A-18E/F Super Hornet.

VFA-94 "Mighty Shrikes" began its transition from the F/A-18C Hornet to the F/A-18F Super Hornet in September 2015, completing the transition in March 2016.

Above: The VFA-94 "Mighty Shrikes" flight line at NAS Lemoore, still assigned to Carrier Air Wing 17.

Below: In June 1990, the "Mighty Shrikes" received its first F/A-18C Hornet and was redesignated VFA-94 on January 1, 1991.

On March 25, 1983, the dawning of the Strike Fighter Squadron era was marked as VA-113 was redesignated VFA-113 and traded the aging A-7 Corsair for the brand-new F/A-18 Hornet. The squadron completed the historic transition to the new multi-role Hornet and on December 14, 1983, became the first fleet operational combat ready Strike Fighter Squadron in the US Navy operating the F/A-18A.

Above: VFA-97 "Warhawks" was formed in 1968, operating the A-7A Corsair. The squadron completed its transition to the F/A-18A on January 24, 1991, and operated the Legacy Hornet until the end of 2013, when the squadron started the conversion to the F/A-18E Super Hornet.

Below: VA-195 was redesignated VFA-195 on April 1, 1985 and commenced transition to the F/A-18A Hornet. The first of 12 new Lot 8 F/A-18A Hornets were delivered to the squadron in October 1985. The "Dambusters" completed its conversion to the F/A-18C Hornet in 1991 and kept operating the last version of the Legacy Hornet until it started its conversion to the F/A-18E Super Hornet in 2010, which was completed early 2011.

Strike Fighter Squadron 137 was formed on July 2, 1985. It received its first Lot 8 F/A-18A Hornets on November 25, 1985. After operating the F/A-18C from 1985 to 2003, VFA-137 "Kestrels" began the transition to the new Lot 25 F/A-18E Super Hornet. After completing the safe-for-flight certification, the "Kestrels" became the third FA-18E squadron in the US Navy. Ten years later, in March 2014, the squadron still operated its Lot 25 F/A-18E Hornets which would be exchanged in 2019 for newer F/A-18Es.

With the conversion from the F-14 Tomcat to the F/A-18E Hornet, VFA-14 "Tophatters" relocated to NAS Lemoore where it still resides today.

Chapter 5

Carrier Air Wing Developments

Carrier air wings became distinct command organizations in July 1938, when the billet for "Commander, Air Group," or "CAG" for short, was authorized. Air wings initially assumed the names of their respective carriers until 1942, when they became numbered.

The USN had ten operational carrier air wings at its disposal after the relatively quiet early years of the 2000s, and in the wake of the very hectic 1990s, in which four carrier air wings were decommissioned. Starting with Carrier Air Wing 13 in 1991, the next air wing to follow was Carrier Air Wing 6, which was decommissioned in 1993. Carrier Air Reserve Wing 30 soon followed in 1994 and, in 1995, Carrier Air Wing 15 was decommissioned. With the replacement of the aging A-6 Intruder and the A-7 Corsair now all integrated and standardized within the F/A-18 Hornet design, the number of carrier air wings was significantly reduced. It was also feared that the F-14 Tomcat's withdrawal from use would result in a further decommissioning of carrier air wings, but, surprisingly, this did not take place since most of the Tomcat squadrons would trade their aircraft for the F/A-18E/F Super Hornet.

Fiscal Year 2017, however, comprised the decommissioning of one carrier air wing as a direct result of several optimization programs. By increasing the efficiency from the optimized fleet response plan, predictable carrier maintenance schedules, increased training phase readiness and fiscal constraints, one CVW could be decommissioned, reducing the remaining operational CVWs total to nine.

CVW-14, based at NAS Lemoore, was selected to be decommissioned in March 2017. As a direct consequence, the active squadrons assigned to CVW-14 were decommissioned or reassigned to other

The adversary aircraft are painted in a wide variety of color schemes. BuNo 761545 is painted in a three-tone brown scheme which is helpful in "blending" the aircraft into the natural environment of the Sierra Nevada where the training exercise range is situated.

CVWs. The Strike Fighter Squadron VFA-15 "Valions," based at NAS Oceana and still equipped with the F/A-18C Legacy Hornets, was decommissioned in the spring of 2017. The second squadron to decommission was VAW-112 "Golden Hawks," equipped with the E-2C Hawkeye and based at NAS Point Mugu, in May 2017. The third squadron was HSC-15 "Red Lions," based at NAS North Island and equipped with MH-60S Helicopters. It was also decommissioned in March 2017. VAQ-134 "Garudas," equipped with the EA-18G and based at NAS Whidbey Island, was not decommissioned, but became a land-based expeditionary squadron and will deploy as detachments in the future. Finally, the planned formation of HSM-76 in 2017 to be equipped with MH-60R helicopters at NAS Jacksonville was canceled. With the decommissioning of VFA-15 "Valions," the remaining Strike Fighter Squadrons were to be aligned between the Atlantic and Pacific commands.

The squadrons that were decommissioned were selected based upon their current training cycle, their situation on conversion to newer types, and their location, with respect to the strategic rebalance and realignment between East Coast and West Coast capabilities. As a direct consequence, the time between deployments for the remaining CVWs decreased.

With the delayed IOC of the F-35C, the Navy was confronted with several operational readiness gaps and, as a result, a number of Legacy Hornets were submitted to a severe refurbishment program in order to extend their operational lifetime. In FY2017, budget request funding was included to bridge the gap between the older Legacy Hornets and the F-35C.

Left: During a large force exercise, VFC-13 launches different formations to challenge the "Blue Air" assets. An average mission might take up to one-and-a-half hours and, during that time, 2–3 launches usually take place.

Below: On July 1, 2003, VF-2 was redesignated VFA-2, and began the transition to the F/A-18F Super Hornet, receiving its first aircraft on October 6, 2003. As of 2021, the squadron has transitioned to the newer Block II F/A-18F Super Hornet equipped with the AESA radar, assigned to Carrier Air Wing 2.

Carrier Air Wing overview

Abbreviation	Modex	Full Name	Location	Emblem
CVW-1	AB	Carrier Air Wing 1	Naval Air Station Oceana, Virginia	
CVW-2	NE	Carrier Air Wing 2	Naval Air Station Lemoore, California	
CVW-3	AC	Carrier Air Wing 3	Naval Air Station Oceana, Virginia	
RCVW-4	AD	Readiness Carrier Air Wing 4	Decommissioned June 1, 1970	
CVW-5	NF	Carrier Air Wing 5	Naval Air Facility Atsugi, Japan	
CVW-6	AE	Carrier Air Wing 6	Decommissioned April 1, 1993	
CVW-7	AG	Carrier Air Wing 7	Naval Air Station Oceana, Virginia	
CVW-8	AJ	Carrier Air Wing 8	Naval Air Station Oceana, Virginia	
CVW-9	NG	Carrier Air Wing 9	Naval Air Station Lemoore, California	
CVW-10	AK NM	Carrier Air Wing 10 Planned 7 Nov 1986	Decommissioned November 20, 1969 Decommissioned June 1, 1988; planned for assignment to USS Independence (CV-62) but never deployed	
CVW-11	NH	Carrier Air Wing 11	Naval Air Station Lemoore, California	
RCVW-12	NJ	Readiness Carrier Air Wing 12	Decommissioned June 30, 1970, modex still in use by Pacific FRS	

Carrier Air Wing overview				
Abbreviation	**Modex**	**Full Name**	**Location**	**Emblem**
CVW-13	*AK*	*Carrier Air Wing 13*	*Decommissioned January 1, 1991*	
CVW-14	*NK*	*Carrier Air Wing 14*	*Decommissioned March 31, 2017*	
CVW-15	*NL*	*Carrier Air Wing 15*	*Decommissioned March 31, 1995*	
CVW-16	*AH*	*Carrier Air Wing 16*	*Decommissioned June 30, 1970*	
CVW-17	NA	Carrier Air Wing 17	Naval Air Station Lemoore, California	
CVW-19	*NM*	*Carrier Air Wing 19*	*Decommissioned June 30, 1977*	
CVWR-20	AF	Carrier Air Wing Reserve 20	Established as CVWR-20 on April 1, 1970, redesignated Tactical Support Wing (TSW), April 1, 2007	
CVW-21	*NP*	*Carrier Air Wing 21*	*Decommissioned December 12, 1975*	
CVWR-30	*ND*	*Carrier Air Wing Reserve 30*	*Decommissioned December 31, 1994*	

As a direct result, the carrier air wing deployment durations were increased from 2011 onwards. From an average of 6.4 months duration between 2008 and 2011, the average duration of a deployment increased to approximately 8.2 months between 2012 and 2014. The average duration of a deployment over the remaining carrier air wings in 2015 was approximately 9 months.

The continued high operational strain resulted in an extended time required for maintenance to deal with the corrosion wear on the aircraft. In addition, the training program for new pilots was delayed as an effect of the increased operational tempo. Additional budget was requested to deal with those challenges, but it also created significant challenges later in the decade. The decommissioning of CVW-14 would only marginally decrease the strike fighter capability gap since the serviceable F/A-18 aircraft were assigned to the remaining active squadrons.

By the end of 2020, the West Coast Carrier Air Wings assigned to the COMNAVAIRPAC comprised the following assets:

COMNAVAIRPAC			
Air Wing	Modex	Carrier designation	Carrier name	Emblem
CVW-2	NE	CVN-70	USS *Carl Vinson*	
CVW-5	NF	CVN-76	USS *Ronald Reagan*	
CVW-9	NG	CVN-75	USS *John C. Stennis*	
CVW-11	NH	CVN-71	USS *Theodore Roosevelt*	
CVW-17	NA	CVN-68	USS *Nimitz*	

All aircraft carriers, naval aircraft, and aviation activities assigned to the Pacific Fleet are under the administrative control of COMNAVAIRPAC. COMNAVAIRPAC is the direct representative of, and the principal advisor to, the Commander in Chief, US Pacific Fleet for the operation, support, and administration of Naval Aviation in the Pacific. The mission of COMNAVAIRPAC is to support the United States Pacific Fleet and the Unified Commands, by providing combat capable Naval Aviation forces which are fully trained, properly manned, interoperable, well maintained, and supported. The official mission of the carrier air wings is to, when ordered, conduct and coordinate offensive and defensive air operations; attack air, surface and subsurface targets afloat and ashore; and provide support to other forces within the capabilities of the aircraft assigned.

Carrier Air Wing 2 (CVW-2) NE		
Squadron	Aircraft	Emblem
VFA-2 "Bounty Hunters"	F/A-18F	
VFA-113 "Stingers"	F/A-18E	
VFA-147 "Argonauts"	F-35C	
VFA-192 "Golden Dragons"	F/A-18E	
VAQ-136 "'Gauntlets"	EA-18G	

Carrier Air Wing 2 (CVW-2) NE		
Squadron	Aircraft	Emblem
VAW-113 "Black Eagles"	E-2D	
HSC-4 "Black Knights"	MH-60S	
HSM-78 "Blue Hawks"	MH-60R	
VRM-30 "Titans"	CMV-22B	

Originally formed as Battle Air Group 74 (CVBG-74) on May 1, 1945, the air wing was renamed Battle Air Group 1 on November 15, 1946. In 1948, it was renamed again as CVG-2, and eventually was redesignated as CVW-2 on December 20, 1963, when the Navy redesignated all the Carrier Air Groups to Carrier Air Wings. The motto of Carrier Air Wing 2 is "For liberty, we fight." Carrier Air Wing 2 was the first air wing with an operational Naval Strike Fighter Squadron equipped with the F-35C, when VFA-147 "Argonauts" transferred from Carrier Air Wing 11 to Carrier Air Wing 2 on March 1, 2019.

With Carrier Airborne Early Warning Squadron VAW-113 already completing their conversion to the E-2D Hawkeye, Carrier Air Wing 2 is one of two air wings that has the disposal of the F-35C within their inventory, although Carrier Air Wing 9 is equipped with a Marines F-35C squadron.

The "Mighty Shrikes" began its transition from the F/A-18C Hornet to the F/A-18F Super Hornet in September 2015, completing the transition in March 2016. In 2019, the squadron changed its modex sequence from NA-4xx to NA-2xx.

Carrier Air Wing 5 (CVW-5) NF		
Squadron	**Aircraft**	**Emblem**
VFA-27 "Royal Maces"	F/A-18E	
VFA-102 "Diamondbacks"	F/A-18F	
VFA-115 "Eagles"	F/A-18E	
VFA-195 "Dambusters"	F/A-18E	
VAQ-141 "Shadowhawks"	EA-18G	
VAW-125 "Torchbearers" "Tigertails"	E-2D	
HSC-12 "Golden Falcons"	MH-60S	
HSM-77 "Saberhawks"	MH-60R	
VRC-30 det.5 "Providers"	C-2A	

In 2019, VFA-14 "Tophatters" celebrated its 100th anniversary. Also referred to as the "Oldest and Boldest," the squadron now operates the F/A-18E and is assigned to Carrier Air Wing 9. F/A-18E BuNo 166428 was passed on to VFA-146 in March 2015.

Carrier Air Wing 5 is based at MCAS Iwakuni and currently operates from CVN-76 USS *Ronald Reagan*. Carrier Air Wing 5 was formed in 1943 as CVG-5 and was redesignated to CVW-5 on December 20, 1963. On January 14, 2014, the US Navy announced that CVN-76 USS *Ronald Reagan* would replace CVN-73 USS *George Washington* as the flagship of Carrier Strike Group 5. Carrier Air Wing 5 continued to be assigned to Carrier Strike Group 5. In August 2015, Carrier Air Wing 5 cross-decked to USS *Ronald Reagan* at San Diego. In October 2015, USS *Ronald Reagan* and CVW-5 moved to their new home base of Kanagawa Prefecture, Japan. The carrier was home-ported at Yokosuka and CVW-5 at Atsugi Naval Air Facility.

Carrier Airborne Early Warning Squadron VAW-125 already completed its conversion to the E-2D Hawkeye in 2014, prior to moving to Carrier Air Wing 5.

In 2015, VFA-146 started its conversion from the F/A-18C to the F/A-18E Super Hornet. In 2020, VFA-146 was assigned to Carrier Air Wing 11, deployed aboard USS *Theodore Roosevelt*.

Fleet Logistics Support Squadron 30 or VRC-30, also referred to as the "Providers," is based at Naval Air Station North Island consisting of five detachments. VRC-30 is one of only two active carrier-capable Fleet Logistics Support squadrons, the other being VRC-40. With a remarkable career within the United States Navy, the aircraft is due for replacement by the CMV-22B Osprey.

Carrier Air Wing Developments

Carrier Air Wing 9 (CVW-9) NG		
Squadron	**Aircraft**	**Emblem**
VFA-14 "Tophatters"	F/A-18E	
VFA-41 "Black Aces"	F/A-18F	
VFA-151 "Vigilantes"	F/A-18E	
VMFA-314 "Black Knights"	F-35C	
VAQ-133 "Wizards"	EA-18G	
VAW-117 "Wallbangers"	E-2D	
HSC-14 "Chargers"	MH-60S	
HSM-71 "Raptors"	MH-60R	
VRC-30 "Providers"	C-2A	

In June 2017, VFA-2 returned to NAS Lemoore after a WesPac cruise on board the CVN-70 *Carl Vinson*. BuNo 166668, modex NE-102, shows the wear after a six-month period at sea.

CVG-9 was established in 1952 and redesignated CVW-9 on December 20, 1963. Currently the air wing consists of eight squadrons, including a fleet logistics multi-mission squadron detachment. CVW-9 has evolved into the most modern carrier-borne strike force in the world, with the addition of the Marine Corps VMFA-314 "Black Knights" squadron operating the F-35C Lightning II, as a replacement of VFA-97 "Warhawks." With the delay in F-35C deliveries, VFA-97 "Warhawks" is scheduled to make the transition to the F-35C in 2021, currently operating its F/A-18E Super Hornets in an adversary role.

Early Warning Squadron 117 also completed its conversion to the E-2D Hawkeye enhancing the early warning capabilities of the air wing.

Carrier Air Wing 11		
Squadron	Aircraft	Emblem
VFA-31 "Tomcatters"	F/A-18E	
VFA-87 "Golden Warriors"	F/A-18E	
VFA-146 "Blue Diamonds"	F/A-18E	
VFA-154 "Black Knights"	F/A-18F	
VAQ-142 "Gray Wolves"	EA-18G	
VAW-115 "Liberty Bells"	E-2C-2000	
HSC-8 "Eightballers"	MH-60S	
HSM-75 "Wolfpack"	MH-60R	
VRC-30. Det.3 "Providers"	C-2A	

Carrier Air Wing 11, previously designated Carrier Air Group Eleven (CVG-11) and (CVAG-11), was formed on Navy Day, October 10, 1942. On December 20, 1963, CVG-11 became Carrier Air Wing 11 (CVW-11).

CVW-11 currently comprises eight squadrons and one logistics detachment. The Strike Fighter Squadrons are all equipped with the F/A-18 Super Hornet and it has a fifty-fifty mix of Atlantic- and Pacific-based squadrons. VFA-146 "Blue Diamonds," operating the F/A-18E, and VFA-154 "Black

Knights," operating the F/A-18F, are based at NAS Lemoore, while VFA-31 "Tomcatters" and VFA-87 "Golden Warriors," both operating the F/A-18E, are based at NAS Oceana.

VAW-115 is equipped with the E-2D AEW aircraft, having completed its conversion from the E-2C-2000 to the E-2D in 2020. Both helicopter squadrons are based at NAS North Island.

Carrier Air Wing 17		
Squadron	**Aircraft**	**Emblem**
VFA-22 "Fighting Redcocks"	F/A-18F	
VFA-94 "Mighty Shrikes"	F/A-18F	
VFA-137 "Kestrels"	F/A-18E	
VMFA-323 "Death Rattlers"	F/A-18C	
VAQ-139 "Cougars"	EA-18G	
VAW-116 "Sun Kings"	E-2C-2000	
HSC-6 "Indians"	MH-60S	
HSM-73 "Battlecats"	MH-60R	
VRC-30 "Providers"	C-2A	

The air group that would evolve into Carrier Air Wing 17 was formed as Carrier Air Group 82 on April 1, 1944. After World War Two, the air group was redesignated to Carrier Air Group 17 (CVAG-17) and redeployed to the East Coast in 1946.

Carrier Air Group 17 was deactivated in September 1958 but was then reactivated in November 1966 as Carrier Air Wing 17 (CVW-17) and assigned to the USS *Forrestal* (CV-59). Just six and a half months after re-forming, the air wing deployed to the Tonkin Gulf aboard USS *Forrestal*. In 2016, CVW-17 was reassigned to CVN-71 USS *Theodore Roosevelt* and in 2019, CVW-17 was again reassigned to CVN-68 USS *Nimitz*.

By the end of 2020, CVW-17 was the last remaining COMNAVAIRPAC still equipped with the F/A-18C Legacy Hornets, assigned to the Marine Corps VMFA-323 "Death Rattlers." With the readiness recovery project completed, it is expected that the Marines squadron will be replaced by an active Naval Strike Fighter Squadron.

Above and below: VF-14 was redesignated to VFA-14 on December 1, 2001, when the squadron transferred to the F/A-18E Super Hornet. The original received batch of F/A-18E Hornets were exchanged with the newer Lot 35 and Lot 37 Super Hornets acquired in FY2013.

At the Landing Signals Officer shack position at NAS Lemoore, the crews train their carrier deck landing skills. BuNo 166811 modex NE-111 performs several touch and goes during their training cycle in October 2018.

Above: BuNo 168484 modex NG-213 is part of Lot 35, acquired under FY2011 and formerly assigned to VFA-106 "Gladiators." It was assigned modex AD-133 from May 2014 until February 2015, when the aircraft was transferred to VFA-14.

Below: Following a successful combat deployment in support of Operation *Enduring Freedom* in 2012, VFA-25 returned to NAS Lemoore to transition to the F/A-18E Super Hornet, completing the transition in late January 2013 and being reassigned to CVW-9. In the fall of 2012, VFA-25 started its transition to the F/A-18E Super Hornet. As part of its transition, VFA-25 joined Carrier Air Wing 9 onboard CVN-74 USS *John C. Stennis*, in 2013.

VFA-86, also known as the "Sidewinders," is a United States Navy F/A-18E Super Hornet squadron based at NAS Lemoore. Its current tail code is AG and its callsign is "Winder." The "Sidewinders" are assigned to Carrier Air Wing 7, performing a variety of combat and support missions aboard the CVN-72 USS *Abraham Lincoln* during 2019.

Preparing for its last cruise assigned to Carrier Air Wing 17, VFA-113 completed its pre-deployment training at NAS Fallon in June 2017. On October 6, 2017, VFA-113 embarked aboard CVN-71 USS *Theodore Roosevelt* to the Western Pacific and Middle East. While deployed, it operated in support of operations *Inherent Resolve* and *Freedom's Sentinel*, returning in May 2018.

VFA-146 "Blue Diamonds" is a United States Navy operational fleet strike fighter squadron based at NAS Lemoore. The squadron operates the F/A-18E Super Hornet and is attached to Carrier Air Wing 11, deployed aboard CVN-71 USS *Theodore Roosevelt*. Its tailcode is NH and the squadron uses radio callsign "Diamond."

The F/A-18 Hornets previously assigned to FRS VFA-125 "Rough Raiders" were all transferred to VFA-122 "Flying Eagles". VFA-125 was deactivated on October 1, 2010, until the squadron was reactivated as the West Coast F-35C FRS on January 12, 2017.

Above: VFA-151 "Vigilantes" is a United States Navy F/A-18E Super Hornet fighter squadron stationed at NAS Lemoore, California. The squadron is a part of Carrier Air Wing 9. As part of CVW-9, the squadron's tail code is NG and the squadron uses radio callsign "Ugly."

Below: VFA-151 began transitioning to Lot 35/36 F/A-18E Super Hornets in February 2013. With the transition, the squadron left Carrier Air Wing 2 and moved to Carrier Air Wing 9 attached to CVN-74 USS *John C. Stennis* on June 1, 2013.

TW-2 regularly deploys to NAF El Centro to provide primary flight training in a constant and stable climate.

The VFA-97 "Warhawks" flight line when the squadron was still operating the F/A-18E assigned to Carrier Air Wing 9 in 2018.

NAS North Island

Group	Squadrons	Aircraft	Modex	Emblem
COMHSMWINGPAC	HSM-71 Helicopter Maritime Strike Squadron 71 "Raptors"	MH-60R	NG-7xx	
	HSM-73 Helicopter Maritime Strike Squadron 73 "Battlecats"	MH-60R	NA-7xx	
	HSM-75 Helicopter Maritime Strike Squadron 75 "Wolfpack"	MH-60R	NH-7xx	
	HSM-78 Helicopter Maritime Strike Squadron 78 "Blue Hawks"	MH-60R	NE-7xx	
	HSM-79 Helicopter Maritime Strike Squadron 79 "Griffins"	MH-60R	AG-7xx	
COMFLELOGSUPPWING	VR-57 Fleet Logistics Support Squadron 57 "Conquistadors"	C-40A	(RX)-xxx	
COMACCLOG	VRC-30 *Fleet Replacement Squadron* "Providers"	C-2A	RW-xxx	
	VRM-30 "Titans"	CMV-22B		
	VRM-50 *Fleet Replacement Squadron* "Foo Dogs"	CMV-22B		

NAS North Island

Group	Squadrons	Aircraft	Modex	Emblem
COMHSCWINGPAC	HSC-4 Helicopter Sea Combat Squadron 4 "Black Knights"	MH-60S	NE-61x	
	HSC-6 Helicopter Sea Combat Squadron 6 "Screaming Indians"	MH-60S	NA-x	
	HSC-8 Helicopter Sea Combat Squadron 8 "Eightballers"	MH-60S	NH-61x	
	HSC-14 Helicopter Sea Combat Squadron 14 "Chargers"	MH-60S	NG-xx	
	HSC-15 Helicopter Sea Combat Squadron 15 "Red Lions" *Decommissioned March 31, 2017*	MH-60S	NA-6xx	
	HSC-21 Helicopter Sea Combat Squadron 21 "Blackjacks"	MH-60S	VR-xx	
	HSC-23 Helicopter Sea Combat Squadron 23 "Wildcards"	MH-60S	WC-4x	
COMHELWINGRES	HSC-85 Helicopter Sea Combat Squadron 85 "Firehawks"	HH-60H MH-60S	NW-xxx	
COMHSMWINGPAC	HSM-35 Helicopter Maritime Strike Squadron 35 "Magicians"	MH-60R MQ-8B	TG-3x	
	HSM-41 Helicopter Maritime Strike Squadron 41 *Fleet Replacement Squadron* "Seahawks"	MH-60R	TS-4xx	
	HSM-49 Helicopter Maritime Strike Squadron 49 "Scorpions"	MH-60R	TX-xxx	

 *NAS Fallon Van Voorhis Field*

Group	Squadrons	Aircraft	Modex	Emblem
CVWR-20	VFC-13 Composite Fighter Squadron 13 "Saints"	F-5F F-5N	AF-xx	
COMSTRKFIGHTWINGPAC	SFWPD Strike Fighter Wing Pacific Detachment "Desert Outlaws"	F/A-18C F/A-18E F/A-18F	AD-xxx NJ-xxx	
NAWDC	NAWDC "Top Gun" "Strike"	E-2C F-16A F-16B F/A-18A F/A-18C F/A-18E F/A-18F E/A-18G MH-60S	10x 11x 0x 2x 3x 3x 4x 5x 6x 7x 50x 60x	
NAS Fallon	Base Flight "Longhorns"	MH-60S	7H-xx	

 *NAS North Island*

Group	Squadrons	Aircraft	Modex	Emblem
COMHSCWINGPAC	HSC-3 Helicopter Sea Combat Squadron 3 Fleet Replacement Squadron "Merlins"	MH-60S	SA-xxx	

 *NAS Kingsville*

Group	Squadrons	Aircraft	Modex	Emblem
TAW-2	VT-21 Training Squadron 21 "Red Hawks"	T-45C	B-xxx	
	VT-22 Training Squadron 22 "Golden Eagles"	T-45C	B-xxx	

 *NAS Corpus Christi*

Group	Squadrons	Aircraft	Modex	Emblem
TAW-4	VT-27 Training Squadron 27 "Boomers"	T-6B	G-xxx	
	VT-28 Training Squadron 28 "Rangers"	T-6B	G-xxx	
	VT-31 Training Squadron 31 "Wise Owls"	T-44C	G-4xx	
	VT-35 Training Squadron 35 "Stingrays"	T-44C	G-4xx	

Edwards AFB (CA)

Group	Squadrons	Aircraft	Modex	Emblem
COMOPTEVFOR	VX-9 Air Test and Evaluation Squadron 9 Det Edwards "Vampires"	F-35C	XE-10x	

Kaneohe Bay MCAF Marion E. Carl Field

Group	Squadrons	Aircraft	Modex	Emblem
CINCPAC	COMPACFLT/FLSW ETD	C-37A		
COMHSMWINGPAC	HSM-37 Helicopter Maritime Strike Squadron 37 "Easy Riders"	MH-60R	TH-xx	
CPRW-2	VPU-2 Patrol Squadron Special Projects Unit 2 "Wizards"	P-3C		
	VP-4 Patrol Squadron 4 Det Kaneohe Bay "Skinny Dragons"	P-8A	YD-xxx	
COMFLELOGSUPPWING	VR-51 Fleet Logistics Support Squadron 51 "Windjammers"	C-40A	RG-xxx	

West Coast Air Bases

	NJRB Fort Worth 			
Group	**Squadrons**	**Aircraft**	**Modex**	**Emblem**
COMFLELOGSUPPWING	VR-59 Fleet Logistics Support Squadron 59 "The Lone Star Express"	C-40A	RY-xxx	

	MCAS Iwakuni 			
Group	**Squadrons**	**Aircraft**	**Modex**	**Emblem**
COMVAQWINGPAC	VAQ-141 Electronic Attack Squadron 141 "Shadowhawks"	EA-18G	NF-5xx	
COMACCLOG	Carrier Airborne Early Warning Squadron 125 VAW-125 "Tigertails"	E-2D	NF-6xx	
	Fleet Logistics Support Squadron VRC-30 Det 5 "Providers"	C-2A	NF-3x	
COMSTRKFIGHTWINGPAC	VFA-27 Strike Fighter Squadron 27 "Royal Maces"	F/A-18E	NF-2xx	
	VFA-102 Strike Fighter Squadron 102 "Diamondbacks"	F/A-18F	NF-1xx	
	VFA-115 Strike Fighter Squadron 115 "Eagles"	F/A-18E	NF-3xx	
	VFA-195 Strike Fighter Squadron 195 "Dambusters"	F/A-18E	NF-4xx	

NAS Point Mugu

Group	Squadrons	Aircraft	Modex	Emblem
COMHSMWINGPAC	VTUAV Maintenance Detachment	MQ-8B/C		
COMACCLOG	VAW-112 Carrier Airborne Early Warning Squadron 112 "Golden Hawks" *Decommissioned May 31, 2017*	E-2C	NG-60x	
	VAW-113 Carrier Airborne Early Warning Squadron 113 "Black Eagles"	E-2D	NE-60x	
	VAW-115 Carrier Airborne Early Warning Squadron 115 "Liberty Bell"	E-2C	NH-60x	
	VAW-116 Carrier Airborne Early Warning Squadron 116 "Sun Kings"	E-2C-II	NA-60x	
	VAW-117 Carrier Airborne Early Warning Squadron 117 "Wallbangers"	E-2D	NG-60x	
CPRW-11	VUP-19 Det. Point Mugu "Big Red"	MQ-4C	PE-xx	
COMFLELOGSUPPWING	VR-55 Fleet Logistics Support Squadron 55 "Bicentennial Minuteman"	C-130T	RU-xxx	
NAWDC	VX-30 Air Test and Evaluation Squadron 30 "Bloodhounds"	NC-37B P-3C, NP-3D KC-130T	BH-1xx 3xx 4xx	

 *NAS Whidbey Island*

Group	Squadrons	Aircraft	Modex	Emblem
CPRW-10	VP-1 Patrol Squadron 1 "Screaming Eagles"	P-8A	YB-xxx	
	VP-4 Patrol Squadron 4 "Skinny Dragons"	P-8A	YD-xxx	
	VP-9 Patrol Squadron 9 "Golden Eagles"	P-8A	PD-xxx	
	VP-40 Patrol Squadron 40 "Fighting Marlins"	P-8A	QE-xxx	
	VP-46 Patrol Squadron 46 "Grey Knights"	P-8A	RC-xxx	
	VP-47 Patrol Squadron 47 "Golden Swordsmen"	P-8A	RD-xxx	
	VUP-11 Unmanned Patrol Squadron 11 "Pegasus"	MQ-4C	LE-xxx	
	VQ-1 Fleet Air Reconnaissance Squadron 1 "World Watchers"	EP-3E P-3C	PR-xxx	
COMRESPATWING	VP-69 Patrol Squadron 69 "Totems"	P-3C	PJ-xxx	
	NAS Whidbey Island Base Flight	MH-60S	FW	

NAS Whidbey Island

Group	Squadrons	Aircraft	Modex	Emblem
COMVAQWINGPAC	VAQ-136 Electronic Attack Squadron 136 "Gauntlets"	EA-18G	NE-50x	
	VAQ-137 Electronic Attack Squadron 137 "Rooks"	EA-18G	AB-50x	
	VAQ-138 Electronic Attack Squadron 138 Joint Expeditionary Squadron "Yellow Jackets"	EA-18G	NL-51x	
	VAQ-139 Electronic Attack Squadron 139 "Cougars"	EA-18G	NA-50x	
	VAQ-140 Electronic Attack Squadron 140 "Patriots"	EA-18G	AG-50x	
	VAQ-142 Electronic Attack Squadron 142 "Gray Wolves"	EA-18G	NH-50x	
	VAQ-144 Electronic Attack Squadron 144	EA-18G	To be formed in October 2021	
	VAQ-209 Electronic Attack Squadron 209 "Star Warriors"	EA-18G	AF-50x	
COMFLELOGSUPPWING	VR-61 Fleet Logistics Support Squadron 61 "Islanders"	C-40A	RS-xxx	

West Coast Air Bases

NAF El Centro

Group	Squadrons	Aircraft	Modex	Emblem
	Detachments	F/A-18C F/A-18D F/A-18E F/A-18F T-45C		

NAS Whidbey Island

Group	Squadrons	Aircraft	Modex	Emblem
COMVAQWINGPAC	VAQ-129 Electronic Attack Squadron 129 *Fleet Replacement Squadron* "New Vikings"	EA-18G	NJ-9xx NJ-5xx	
	VAQ-130 Electronic Attack Squadron 130 "Zappers"	EA-18G	AC-50x	
	VAQ-131 Electronic Attack Squadron 131 Joint Expeditionary Squadron "Lancers"	EA-18G	NE-55x	
	VAQ-132 Electronic Attack Squadron 132 Joint Expeditionary Squadron "Scorpions"	EA-18G	NL-54x	
	VAQ-133 Electronic Attack Squadron 133 "Wizards"	EA-18G	NG-5xx	
	VAQ-134 Electronic Attack Squadron 134 "Garudas"	EA-18G	NL-53x	
	VAQ-135 Electronic Attack Squadron 135 Joint Expeditionary Squadron "Black Ravens"	EA-18G	NL-52X	

NAS Lemoore

Group	Squadron	Aircraft	Modex	Emblem
COMSTRKFIGHTWINGPAC	VFA-137 Strike Fighter Squadron 137 "Kestrels"	F/A-18E	NA-2xx	
	VFA-146 Strike Fighter Squadron 146 "Blue Diamonds"	F/A-18E	NH-3xx	
	VFA-147 Strike Fighter Squadron 147 "Argonauts"	F-35C	NE-4xx	
	VFA-151 Strike Fighter Squadron 151 "Vigilantes"	F/A-18E	NG-4xx	
	VFA-154 Strike Fighter Squadron 154 "Black Knights"	F/A-18F	NH-1xx	
	VFA-192 Strike Fighter Squadron 192 "Golden Dragons"	F/A-18E	NE-xxx	
	Base Flight	MH-60S	7S-xx	

NAWS China Lake (CA) Armitage Field

Group	Squadrons	Aircraft	Modex	Emblem
NAWDC	VX-31 Test and Evaluation Squadron 31 "Dust Devils"	MH-60S F/A-18A/C F/A-18D F/A-18E F/A-18F NEA-18G AV-8B/+/(R) T-39D	DD-1xx DD-11x DD-11x/2xx DD-2xx DD-46x DD-5xx DD-8x	
COMOPTEVFOR	VX-9 Test and Evaluation Squadron 9 "Vampires"	F/A-18C F/A-18D F/A-18E F/A-18F EA-18G	XE-1xx XE-2xx XE-30x XE-40x XE-5xx	

Chapter 6
West Coast Air Bases

NAS Lemoore

Group	Squadron	Aircraft	Modex	Emblem
COMSTRKFIGHTWINGPAC	VFA-2 Strike Fighter Squadron 2 "Bounty Hunters"	F/A-18F	NE-1xx	
	VFA-14 Strike Fighter Squadron 14 "Tophatters"	F/A-18E	NG-2xx	
	VFA-22 Strike Fighter Squadron "Fighting Redcocks"	F/A-18F	NA-1xx	
	VFA-25 Strike Fighter Squadron 25 "Fist of the Fleet"	F/A-18E	AG-4xx	
	VFA-41 Strike Fighter Squadron 41 "Black Aces"	F/A-18F	NG-1xx	
	VFA-86 Strike Fighter Squadron 86 "Sidewinders"	F/A-18E	AG-3xx	
	VFA-94 Strike Fighter Squadron 94 "Mighty Shrikes"	F/A-18E	NA-4xx	
	VFA-97 Strike Fighter Squadron 97 "Warhawks"	F/A-18E	NG-xx	
	VFA-113 Strike Fighter Squadron 113 "Stingers"	F/A-18E	NE-3xx	
	VFA-122 *Fleet Replacement Squadron* "Flying Eagles"	F/A-18E F/A-18F	NJ-1xx NJ-2xx	

West Coast Air Bases

	Tinker AFB			
Group	Squadrons	Aircraft	Modex	Emblem
CSCW-1	VQ-3 Fleet Air Reconnaissance Squadron 3 "Ironmen"	E-6B	TC	
	VQ-4 Fleet Air Reconnaissance Squadron 4 "Shadows"	E-6B	HL	
	VQ-7 Fleet Air Reconnaissance Squadron 7 "Roughnecks"	E-6B		

	Dallas – Love Field			
Group	Squadrons	Aircraft	Modex	Emblem
Naval Air Systems Command-Flight Support Detachment	BUPERS SDC Dallas	P-8A		

VFA-113 "Stingers" was the last Navy F/A-18C legacy squadron on the West Coast to transition to the Super Hornet. On October 6, 2017, VFA-113 embarked aboard USS *Theodore Roosevelt* to the Western Pacific and Middle East. While deployed, it operated in support of operations *Inherent Resolve* and *Freedom's Sentinel*, returning in May 2018. In 2019, the squadron was reassigned from Carrier Air Wing 17 to Carrier Air Wing 2, thus swapping places with VFA-137.

This Super Hornet assigned to VFA-151 "Vigilantes," based at NAS Lemoore, crashed on July 31, 2019, at about 1000hrs in the so-called "Star Wars Canyon." The pilot, LT Charles Walker, did not survive the crash. LT Walker was an incredible naval aviator, husband, and son. He was an integral member of the "Vigilante" family, and his absence was keenly felt on the flight line.

Above: The Lemoore search and rescue squadron has four MH-60S helicopters. Seen here, on the NAS Lemoore flight line, is BuNo 165755 modex 7S-01.

Left: Before NAF Atsugi was abandoned, the base used three UC-12Fs as its base fight liaison aircraft. Seen here is BuNo 163562 landing at NAF Atsugi in early 2016.

NAS Fallon is one of the US Navy's most important locations for aviation training and development. Situated in northwest Nevada, in many ways, Fallon is to US Naval Aviation what Nellis AFB is to the USAF, with many of the units based at the two facilities having similar roles. One thing that both bases certainly do have in common is extensive range facilities. The Fallon Range Training Complex is huge and encompasses four distinctive range areas, including radar and threat simulations and areas for the delivery of live weapons. All versions of the Super Hornet, including the Growler, are added to the NAWDC inventory to project realistic scenarios.

Above: VFA-41 "Black Aces" uses callsign "Fast Eagle." BuNo "Fast Eagle 107" is buzzing through Rainbow Canyon near Father Crowley point captured here during October 2019.

Right: VFA-113 "Stingers" is currently assigned to Carrier Air Wing 2. The squadron transferred from Carrier Air Wing 17 to Carrier Air Wing 2, exchanging places with VFA-137.

Below: On July 15, 2018, VFA-113 "Stingers" celebrated its 70th anniversary assigned to Carrier Air Wing 17.

US Naval Air Power: West Coast 2010–20

Above: It is not a common thing to experience a rainy day at NAS Lemoore. Seen here just after a rain shower is BuNo 165794 modex NJ-104, with a beautiful reflection on the concrete surface.

Left: In the summer of 2016, VFA-136 was moved from NAS Oceana to NAS Lemoore but remained with Carrier Air Wing 1 until October 1, 2020.

VFA-136 was established on July 1, 1985, at NAS Lemoore, California, under the instruction of VFA-125. The squadron received its first F/A-18A Hornet on January 7, 1986, and a month later it moved to its new homeport of NAS Cecil Field, Florida. The squadron's "Knighthawk" insignia and nickname were approved by Chief of Naval Operations on May 23, 1985 and have remained unchanged.

Right: On December 15, 2009, VFA-192 departed NAF Atsugi and CVW-5 as part of a homeport change to NAS Lemoore and CVW-9. Likewise, VFA-115 arrived in NAF Atsugi on December 13, 2009, to be the replacement squadron for VFA-192. Upon arrival at NAS Lemoore, VFA-192 joined CVW-9.

Below: VFA-154 "Black Knights" transferred to its current air wing, Carrier Air Wing 11, in 2012 and twice deployed aboard CVN-68 USS *Nimitz*. The "Black Knights" is currently honing its skills and strengthening its resolve with Carrier Air Wing 11 and CVN-71 USS *Theodore Roosevelt*.

During late 2010, the VFA-195 "Dambusters" transitioned to the F/A-18E Super Hornet. In late 2015, Carrier Air Wing 5 was scheduled to be transferred to CVN-76 USS *Ronald Reagan*, which replaced CVN-73 USS *George Washington* as the Navy's forward deployed aircraft carrier at Yokosuka, Japan.

Chapter 7
Naval Strike Fighter Developments

The war against terrorism put enormous strain on the Super Hornet's operational employability over the last few years. This resulted in an actual Naval Aviation Strike Fighter readiness crisis in the aftermath of the conflict. A major maintenance backlog presented itself, and the Navy worked intensively to decrease the number of Super Hornets marked as "non-mission capable." In November 2017, Vice Admiral Mike Shoemaker stated that nearly one in three Hornets were non-operational and awaiting serious overdue maintenance. Later in 2017, the United States Secretary of the Navy stated that only one-third of the more than 546 Super Hornets within the operational inventory of the US Naval fleet were mission capable and considered fit for deployment. Those classed as not fit for deployment were either in the process of maintenance, awaiting maintenance, or were assigned to the training squadrons, since their condition allowed the aircraft only to be used for training purposes.

During the "low-point" of the crisis, unusual measures were deemed necessary. To meet the requirements of the planned deployments for the 2018 carrier strike groups of the USS *Carl Vinson*, USS *Nimitz*, and USS *Theodore Roosevelt*, a total of 94 Super Hornets had to be submitted for overdue maintenance at the Naval depots. Until very recently, the Navy struggled to close the readiness requirements gap and continued to develop projects to prevent similar situations in the future.

Super Hornet Combat Readiness Setbacks

With the readiness crisis in progress, the delivery of factory new Super Hornets was still in full swing, with the Hornet production line planning to remain open until at least 2025. In March 2018, Kuwait ordered 22 F/A-18Es and six F/A-18Fs and the US Navy ordered an additional ten Super Hornets, on top of the 14 aircraft already purchased in FY2018. The 2019 defense budget was expected to include the acquisition of 110 additional Super Hornets, to be delivered in FY2019–23.

Although all operational active Naval Strike Fighter Squadrons completed their conversions to the Super Hornet during 2018, Carrier Air Wing 14 was decommissioned in March 2017. This reduced

BuNo 165675 has spent its entire operational career with VFA-122. The aircraft, assigned construction number 1510/F014, is an F/A-18F Block 53 Rhino ordered in FY1998 and delivered to the Navy in June 2000, here presented as modex NJ-103.

the number of active carrier air wings to nine, but the delivery of additional Super Hornets was still deemed necessary. Due to the decommissioning of CVW-14, one squadron, VFA-15 "Valions" was decommissioned on June 12, 2017. The decommissioning of CVW-14, however, only marginally decreased the Strike Fighter availability gap.

Another reason for the operational readiness gap was the increase in the carrier air wing deployment durations, which had been increasing from 2011 onwards. The long deployments combined with the continuing high operational strain resulted in an extended time required for maintenance to deal with the corrosive wear on the aircraft. Furthermore, the difficulties in maintaining the operational fleet, due to a shortage of critical spare parts, resulted in a significant backlog of Super Hornets that could not be classified as combat capable.

The requirement for fleet maintenance received a higher priority due to the delayed IOC of the F-35C Lightning II, which led to the USN being confronted with an increased number of operational readiness gaps. As a result, several operational Legacy Hornets were submitted to a severe refurbishment program to extend their operational lifetime. This was the main reason funding was requested from FY2017 onwards, to bridge the gap between the older Legacy Hornets and the F-35C Lightning II.

Situation Appraisal

With the knowledge that the War on Terror had resulted in a heavily "crippled" Super Hornet availability, the Navy completed a situation appraisal, in order to conduct an analysis of the root cause of the situation. Besides the high tempo of operations and the strain on the aircraft and aircrews, economic restrictions, as an effect of budget cutbacks, also played a vital role.

Early in 2017, the Navy provided Boeing with two carefully selected Super Hornets, both possessing the highest amount of flight hours, to facilitate the situation appraisal and gain an understanding of the scope of work to be expected in overhauling the Super Hornets. It also provided Boeing with an opportunity to determine if the condition of these aircraft matched its expectations, based upon and developed through modeling, simulation, and physical torture testing of various components.

The Navy provided one F/A-18E and one F/A-18F to Boeing for the situation appraisal process. Both sub-types were carefully analyzed and the findings were better than expected. In October 2017, Boeing completed the situation appraisal and, surprisingly, concluded that there were no severe deviations compared to its simulated expectations and the airframes and components were in a far better state than expected.

Assessing Service Life Extension

The Super Hornet design specifications stated an operational lifetime of 6,000 flight hours. Currently, the earliest delivered Super Hornets have reached 35 percent of the hours limit. If this amount of flight hours is extrapolated to the planned service life of the Hornet to 2035, this will not be sufficient to meet the operational commitment expectations. Since this was partially anticipated, the development of a Service Life Assessment Program (SLAP) commenced in 2008 and comprised a three-phased program. The development of this program was completed in early 2018. The main purpose of SLAP was to assess the feasibility of extending the current Super Hornet operational service life from 6,000 flight hours to 9,000 flight hours. It collected data used to analyze the effect of the current use and resulting state of the aircraft. The analyzed data will be compared with structural test data. Subsequently, a Service Life Extension Program (SLEP) should effectively result in the actual prolongation of operational service lifetime of the aircraft until at least 2035.

The first West Coast squadron which made the conversion to the F-35C Lightning II in January 2018 was VFA-147. Initially assigned to Carrier Air Wing 11 modex NH-4xx, the squadron transferred to Carrier Air Wing 2 in March 2019, completed its carrier qualification training, and prepared for its initial deployment on board of USS *Carl Vinson*.

Three stages have been defined to assess each individual airframe. During the first stage, the airframe was assessed, including the flight controls and all integrated subsystems. In the second stage, the data derived from the assessment was analyzed. The results from this stage were the basis for the SLEP, as they specify the modifications and necessary inspections required to maintain and ensure airworthiness. The third stage was carrying out the defined work as assessed in the analysis. The first Super Hornet that was overhauled by SLEP commenced in 2015. Work was carried out by Boeing. An increasing number of aircraft are currently in the process of entering stage 2 and stage 3. On an annual basis, 40–50 Super Hornets are submitted to their specific SLEP in the Boeing facilities at St. Louis and San Antonio. Hornets that had been earmarked as "worst condition aircraft" were submitted to this program with priority.

In May 2018, the Defense Logistics Agency awarded a five-year contract to Boeing, budgeted at US$427m annually. This contract comprised the delivery of required spare parts, and the starting point was to work through a reasonable backlog of Hornets due for maintenance. The program was referred to as the "Depot Readiness Initiative" and the main purpose was to drastically decrease the number of non-mission capable Hornets. As a result of this program, during 2018, the operational employability situation slightly improved to 50 percent. By early August 2018, it was reported that 241 aircraft were fully mission capable, and, by the end of August, the number of mission capable aircraft improved to 270 aircraft.

In 2018, US Naval Air Systems Command (NAVAIR) also awarded a US$17m contract to Boeing for the conversion of 11 existing Super Hornets for the Blue Angels. The contract comprised the retrofit documentation and kits for nine F/A-18E and two F/A-18F aircraft, in accordance with engineering change proposal 6480. The retrofit was carried out in the St. Louis facility and completed in early 2021. The Blue Angels received their first Hornets in 1986 and operated all variants of the Legacy Hornet and received refurbished Super Hornets throughout 2020.

Legacy Hornets' Last Leap

The first F/A-18C models entered service in 1987 and cost US$29m each. The US Navy retired most of the Legacy Hornets from operational deployment, as the F-35C neared operational status. The last Legacy Hornet cruise took place on the USS *Carl Vinson* and was completed on March 12, 2018. The last squadron operating the F/A-18C was VFA-34 "Blue Blasters" and it started its conversion to the F/A-18E Hornet upon its return. On February 1, 2018, the last Legacy Hornet operations took place at NAS Oceana, where VFA-34 was the last squadron to exchange its Legacy Hornets for Super Hornets. On April 17, 2020, the Navy took delivery of its final Boeing F/A-18E Block II Super Hornet. The aircraft, with construction number E322, was the last of 322 single-seat F/A-18E and 286 two-seat F/A-18F jets delivered since 2005, and was delivered to "Blue Blasters."

By 2020, the role of the Legacy Hornet within the Navy, however, was completed, and it will continue service only with the NAWDC at NAS Fallon, and possibly in reserve squadron VFA-204 "River Rattlers."

It was concluded that 136 F/A-18D aircraft that reside within the US Navy and US Marine Corps could be authorized to be struck of charge. This decision was taken because their effective technical lifetime was exceeded, and it would require significant funding to extend their service life through refurbishment and refit programs. The decision to withdraw these aircraft from use was mainly based upon the readiness risk and long-term operational costs to keep the aircraft combat capable versus the gain in capability compared to the Super Hornet.

Withdrawing the F/A-18D from service and putting them in long-term storage also helped keep the Legacy Hornets in use within the US Marine Corps, using them for parts and sending any usable aircraft to the Marine operational squadrons. In March 2018, the US Navy revealed that the 136 selected F/A-18D aircraft would be sent to the 309th AMARG at Davis-Monthan AFB to serve as parts donors for the remaining Legacy Hornets within the US Navy and US Marine Corps.

On March 6, 2018, the plan to strike the F/A-18D from the operational inventory between FY2017–20 was approved by the US Navy.

On January 17, 2019, Raytheon received a purchase order to supply a total of 84 US Marine Corps Legacy Hornets with new APG-79 version 4 Active Electronically Scanned Array (AESA) radar. This radar system was similar to the application implemented in the Super Hornets and was in accordance with the US Marine Corps 2018 Aviation Plan. The delivery of the first modernized Legacy Hornets was delivered in 2020, and it will continue until 2022, as a temporary measure to keep the Legacy Hornets combat capable until they are replaced by the F-35B and F-35C aircraft.

Transferring the Legacy Hornets

According to the United States Marine Corps 2018 Aviation Plan, the service operated 180 Legacy Hornets divided across active, reserve, and training squadrons. Additionally, another 100 Legacy Hornets were all submitted to heavy maintenance.

From 2017 onwards, however, more than 50 percent of all Legacy Hornets within the operational inventory of the US Marine Corps were not in operationally capable status and, therefore, not mission ready. Supplementing the shortage in available Hornet resources, the USMC received 30 Legacy Hornets from the US Navy that had been stored at 309th AMARG at Davis-Monthan AFB. These were returned to active service within the operational squadrons. However, the struggle to keep an increasing number of aircraft in operational status continued.

Just before its deployment in October 2019, VFA-154 received a number of brand-new F/A-18F Super Hornets. This aircraft, BuNo 169654, was newly delivered to the squadron just prior to the carrier air wing training at NAS Fallon and is not seen with the standard Carrier Air Wing 11 NH modex.

With the introduction of the F-35C Lightning II to the operational squadrons, the FRSs were formed to provide the required training to the squadrons making their transition. In May 2012, VFA-101 was the designated East Coast F-35C FRS and former Legacy Hornet FRS VFA-125 was reactivated at NAS Lemoore on January 12, 2017, as the West Coast FRS. It received its first aircraft on January 25, 2017. The aircraft were transferred from VFA-101.

On October 1, 2010, VFA-125, serving as the Hornet FRS, was deactivated, and its aircraft and personnel were merged into VFA-122. The merger was intended to cut administrative costs and streamline training in anticipation of the F/A-18A+, F/A-18C, and F/A-18D Hornets being replaced by the F/A-18E/F Super Hornet and F-35 Lightning II. The "merged" squadron continued operations as VFA-122 "Flying Eagles," while the "Rough Raiders" of VFA-125 was put into "hibernation" until a later date, pending reactivation as an F-35 training squadron.

The F/A-18D aircraft will subsequently be replaced by the F-35B Lightning II. The choice of the US Marine Corps to not select the Super Hornet as an interim solution between the full swing delivery of the F-35 has created severe problems. Unfortunately, the development challenges and delays in deliveries of the F-35C Lightning II have slowed the process of replacing the Legacy Hornets into the operational squadrons. According to current expectations, the US Marine Corps plans to operate the Legacy Hornets until 2030 when the aircraft will be retired.

The hand-me-down aircraft could be a major boost to the US Marine Corps. Depending on whether the US Navy has completely stripped the retired aircraft of useful components, those donor airframes could continue to support Marine Corps Hornets as well. The deciding factor will be how fast the US Navy can transition its own units and transfer the Legacy Hornets to the US Marine Corps squadrons.

Remaining on Top of Things

On March 1, 2018, Boeing stated that the initial SLEP contract to begin the overhaul of four Navy Super Hornets was received. The company said it would open a production line at its San Antonio, Texas, plant specifically for this program in 2019. Boeing combined this traditional service life extension work with the Block III upgrades to try and streamline the integral process. The new configuration included infrared search and track capability, conformal fuel tanks, updated electronic warfare systems, a larger widescreen cockpit display, an improved mission computer, and data links with greater capacity to send and receive information.

Starting the program, Boeing estimated the combined upgrade process would take approximately 18 months per aircraft. However, through gaining experience and efficiency, Boeing expected to decrease the required modification time to 12 months as the facilities at San Antonio came online, and they worked through any residual issues. The first four airframes served as an important trial run, and both Boeing and the Navy had been working together since 2017 to get a better understanding of exactly what the process entailed.

The two parties were eager not to repeat the issues they experienced with an earlier service life extension effort for older F/A-18C/D Hornets that started in 2012. That project suffered extensive delays. This was caused by attempting to do the work as an extension of normal, less intensive, depot-level maintenance. The program hit several unexpected issues, including discovering more extensive structural wear and tear and corrosion than expected, once contractors actually began pulling the aircraft apart.

Alongside the extension of the crippled Super Hornet inventory and the immediate demand for maintenance, the Navy also purchased an additional 110 Super Hornets in FY2019 and awarded Boeing with a contract to start with the overhaul and the SLEP of the existing "early" Super Hornets to the latest Block III configuration.

Block III Modifications

The two-seat Block III Super Hornet includes the following features: integrated conformal fuel tanks, an enhanced electronic suite featuring improved electronic defenses, data links, and other mission systems. The infrared search and track system will further improve the Hornet's already powerful AN/APG-79 active electronically scanned array radar. This enabled the crew to spot adversaries at extended ranges. The conformal fuel tanks increased the overall range without the need for drop tanks, allowing the Hornet to carry additional weapons or other mission specific equipment.

Further improvements, currently in development, include some limited stealth features, such as a fully enclosed weapons pod and a more powerful, fuel-efficient engine. However, these updates are unlikely to be part of the final Block III configuration.

Integrally combining the refurbishment and modification program will most probably result in a multiple phase overhaul for a yet non-defined number of Super Hornets. This may result in an extended overall timeframe to get fully modernized jets fit for deployment service. The full SLEP modification kits, including software, will not be ready until as early as 2022 or 2023. This means that the selected jets in severe need of new parts and maintenance before that period will only get a partial update and will have to return to the factory for the additional modifications when available.

The Path to Success

With deliveries of the newly built Block III Super Hornets, the Navy intends to reduce the most imminent demands and close the gap to the desired level of operational-readiness capable Super Hornets.

On September 10, 2018, the Chief of Naval Operations promulgated the deactivation of VFA-101. On May 23, 2019, VFA-101 completed deactivation and was consolidated into the remaining F-35C FRS, VFA-125 "Rough Raiders." Its assets and support personnel were moved to NAS Lemoore, home of VFA-125. BuNo 169631 here still presents code 106, which was its former code while operating with VFA-101.

Alongside the SLEP, the US Navy has been significantly reducing its Legacy Hornet inventory. This is in favor of operating the advanced Super Hornet alongside the F-35C Lightning II, which is now slowly being integrated into the operational Navy squadrons. The modification program will boost the numbers of Legacy Hornets in the Marine Corps squadrons, thus helping to keep them mission capable until the USMC can acquire sufficient numbers of F-35B Lightning II aircraft.

VFA-147 "Argonauts" was carefully selected as the first operational squadron to make the conversion from the F/A-18E Super Hornet to the F-35C. As the US Navy's first operational F-35C squadron, the "Argonauts" was issued its interim safe-for-flight operations certification status by the Commander Joint Strike Fighter Wing (CJSFW) on October 19, 2018, needing only to independently conduct its carrier qualification to receive the full certification. The finalization of the safe-for-flight operations certification process ensured that the squadron had sufficiently qualified personnel to implement safety and maintenance programs in support of fleet operations. In preparation for the transition to the F-35C Lightning II, the US Navy reactivated Strike Fighter Squadron VFA-125 "Rough Raiders" as the FRS for the aircraft in January 2017.

The "Argonauts" has a long history operating the Legacy Hornet and Super Hornet. It received its initial F/A-18C Hornets on July 20, 1989, and performed its conversion to that platform using the assets of the "Rough Raiders." At the time, VFA-125 was the current FRS for the Hornet. The "Argonauts" received its first Lot XII "Night Attack" Hornets in December 1989. After a deployment to the Persian Gulf in March 1991, in support of Operation *Desert Storm*, VFA-147 became the Navy's first operational F/A-18 squadron to employ the Navigational Forward Looking Infrared pods and night-vision goggles. In June 1995, it completed the transition to new Lot 16/17 F/A-18C aircraft, with the APG-73 radar and enhanced performance engines. In May 1998, the squadron traded its Lot 16 Hornets for Lot 11 Hornets received from VFA-195. The squadron began conversion to the F/A-18E Super Hornet in October 2007 and successfully completed its transition in February 2008.

Operating the F/A-18E Super Hornet, the squadron completed several deployments at a very high pace. During its 2010 pre-deployment workup cycle, the squadron was awarded the 2009 Pacific Arleigh Burke Fleet Trophy for its enormous strides in battle efficiency since its transition to the F/A-18E Super Hornet. In 2013, the "Argonauts" maintenance team won the Golden Wrench Award and the LT J G Bruce Carrier Maintenance Award for the first part of its cruise for outstanding maintenance department and the ability to be the go-to squadron in Carrier Air Wing 11. VFA-147 completed its

VF-2 joined Carrier Air Wing 2 in 1994, operating the F-14D Tomcat. Since the squadron transferred to the F/A-18F Hornet, the squadron has not been reassigned to another carrier air wing. BuNo 166804 modex NE-100 represents the VFA-2 "Bounty Hunters" commander aircraft.

deployment with CVW-11 embarked on USS *Nimitz* (CVN 68) and returned to its home base at NAS Lemoore in December 2017, after a six-month deployment operating the F/A-18E Super Hornet.

Almost immediately after returning home from deployment, the "Argonauts" started the conversion process from the F/A-18E Super Hornet to the F-35C Lightning II. Although some level of training took place at Eglin AFB, most of the training of the maintainers and pilots took place at NAS Lemoore. VFA-147 personnel worked with VFA-125 to complete the required qualifications and syllabus events to gain hands-on experience with the aircraft. Maintaining this new platform required more space, and, as a result, a new larger hangar was built and appointed to the F-35C, which provided sufficient space for the necessary maintenance operations. Currently, additional hangars are scheduled for construction for future additional F-35C squadrons.

VFA-147 received its first aircraft in early October 2018. Since the F-35C does not have a two-seat trainer variant, the basic training principles were provided using the full-mission simulator. For training purposes, several simulators were implemented at NAS Lemoore with additional simulator assets scheduled for delivery as the program grew. AT Chief Joseph Walter of VFA-125 stated, "The simulator is very accurate and resembles the real-time situation to a very high detail." After almost three months of simulator training, on April 18, 2018, VFA-147 carried out its first flight on the F-35C.

With this, the "Argonauts" received its full certification on October 19, 2018. The certification was the final step for the squadron's conversion from F/A-18E Super Hornet to the F-35C Lightning II, and it was one of the crucial steps for the US Navy's F-35C program to obtain IOC in early 2019.

IOC was declared once the full capability of the US Navy's F-35C program was demonstrated and all remaining criteria were met. Once the IOC was acquired, the following steps were toward the successful integration of the aircraft into the fleet. This was completed in February 2019, in preparation for the first deployment of the "Argonauts" in 2021, embarked on CVN-70 USS *Carl Vinson*.

The ambitious plans of the US Navy comprised additional squadrons equipped with the F-35C to operate alongside the F/A-18E/F Super Hornets in the state-of-the-art future Naval Strike Fighter Wing. Although the next squadrons to start the conversion to the F-35C have not yet been selected, construction plans for the new hangar locations at NAS Lemoore have started. The Joint Strike Fighter Wing's focus will be expanding the F-35C capabilities within the US Navy and managing the conversion of all selected squadrons to the new fifth-generation fighter.

VFA-25 "Fist of the Fleet" transferred from Carrier Air Wing 9 to Carrier Air Wing 7 in 2015 and completed its first deployment as part of Carrier Air Wing 7 on the USS *Harry S. Truman* from November 16, 2015, until July 13, 2016.

VFA-27 "Royal Maces" is a United States Navy F/A-18E Super Hornet fighter squadron stationed at MCAS Iwakuni. It is a part of Carrier Air Wing 5 and is attached to the aircraft carrier CVN 76 USS *Ronald Reagan*.

Above left: In September 2003, VF-154 left NAF Atsugi for the last time and ended its 13 years in Japan and 20 years in the Tomcat. A month later, VF-154 was redesignated VFA-154 at its new home at NAS Lemoore and began transitioning to the Navy's newest strike fighter, the F/A-18F Super Hornet.

Above right: Assigned to Carrier Air Wing 9 in October 2018, BuNo 168872 modex NG-305 performs a high-speed run through Rainbow Canyon.

Below: While stationed at Naval Air Station Lemoore, VFA-27 "Royal Maces" transitioned to the F/A-18A Hornet on January 24, 1991, and was officially redesignated Strike Fighter Squadron 27. The squadron emblem was also changed to a green background, white cloud, and silver gauntlet with silver mace. In February 2013, the "Royal Maces" executed a transpacific journey to accept new Lot 34 and 35 F/A-18E Super Hornets to maintain its superior technological abilities in the US Navy's Pacific Fleet.

Chapter 8
Readiness Recovery Developments

While the Navy had been working hard to improve the readiness gap and lessen the maintenance backlog, there were still issues in the fleet. On a few occasions, operational strike squadrons had to swap aircraft with the FRSs in order to have adequate numbers to start a new deployment. By early 2018, according to non-confirmed estimations, the percentage of non-combat capable Super Hornets and Growlers increased from 50 to 66 percent.

Specifying Key Performance Indicators

A major catch-up race was initiated to increase the percentage of mission capable aircraft within the operational squadrons, and priority was given to increase the operational combat capability of the Super Hornet and Growler fleet. The target set by the Commander Naval Air Forces was to reach an 80 percent combat capable Super Hornet and Growler fleet by September 2019.

The definition of the "80 percent mission capable status" was disputed and, in response, it was further specified that the mission capable status only applied to the aircraft marked as operational. However, it remained unclear what was meant by an "operational" status, especially as a non-operational status could apply to aircraft in the process of scheduled maintenance or heavy depot maintenance. Further explanation defined that the operational status of a Super Hornet or Growler included Primary Mission Aircraft Inventory (PMAI) capability, which meant that the aircraft could operate within the nine operational carrier air wing squadrons that form the Naval Aviation tactical air power. Although the Navy also reported a mission capable status of at least 80 percent of its remaining Legacy Hornet fleet, there were no specific reports concerning how it reached that key performance indicator.

A situation appraisal survey performed throughout 2017 and 2018 specified the requirements per aircraft, and the maintenance and supply depots supported by readiness-enabling commands commenced their task to significantly reduce the number of non-combat capable aircraft. The Naval Sustainment System Aviation and Naval Aviation Enterprise commenced developing programs to enhance efficiency of the maintenance service practices, optimizing standards and procedures and work instructions using the experience and input of the commercial industry.

From 2016 onward, the Navy directives stated that the presentation of the Navy squadron commander aircraft should be restricted to a modest presentation. For this purpose, the tails of the CAG birds were limited to an absolute minimum. Seen here is BuNo 168927, which is from a lot of 37 F/A-18Es ordered in FY 2013. It was assigned to VFA-122 as modex NJ-264 between August 2015 and February 2016. In the summer of 2017, the aircraft was assigned to VFA-14 and served as its CAG bird.

As a direct consequence, any reforms deemed necessary were commenced in early 2018. With an increased number of operational Hornets, however, the number of aircraft requiring maintenance increased as well. From 2000 to 2010, the average number of Hornets submitted to the Fleet Readiness Centers varied between 250 and 260 aircraft, but the number has since grown to approximately 320 aircraft per year. With the maintenance backlog, the depot centers were expected to attain the service goals of 341 Super Hornets and 93 Growlers by the end of September 2019, which was an extremely difficult target to meet.

The Smell of Success

The supply chain of management, engineering practices, governance activity, and safety procedures were significantly improved, and, consequently, it became more efficient to get the Super Hornets, and later the Growlers, back on their feet as soon as they could. Since this process proved to be very successful, the lessons learned would be implemented across the remaining types within the operational inventory of the USN.

The tremendous efforts of the squadron maintainers and the Fleet Readiness Centers proved to be the key to meeting the deadlines of the project. As a result of their dedication, 2019 was the first year in which the key performance indicator "aviator flight hour" increased and was the first year in which the Navy was able to perform its allocation of flight hours completely, proving the reforms led to success and were not a "change" for the sake of change. By staying critical to the processes, even further improvements can be realized.

Although the "mission capable" status is not equal to a "full mission capable" status (also referred to as a "Code One Standard," which defines the aircraft as fit to meet any assigned mission requirement) on September 24, 2019, the Commander, Naval Air Forces stated the 80 percent mission capable status goal had been achieved. Additionally, the Navy had managed to hit this performance indicator in a period of 12 months. The goal to have at least 320 Super Hornets in mission capable status was even reached earlier in September 2019.

Another Hurdle to Take

Just when it seemed like the problems of the Super Hornet fleet were overcome, a new hurdle became apparent. Although the 80 percent goal was an important achievement for the Navy, and a significant improvement in availability rates, serious questions remained whether this was, and will remain, a sustainable situation in the long term.

The Navy stated that by 2020 it was able to sustain around 320 mission capable Super Hornets and planned to conduct a short-term readiness surge to reach the intended 340 Super Hornets. How this performance was being sustained remains unclear for the Super Hornet operations.

In June 2019, it became clear there was a shortage of spare parts and that a possible result could be the reduction of operational hours for the operational squadrons. In July, the Navy communicated that this would only be applicable to the Naval Air Force Atlantic resources and would certainly not affect the Super Hornet fleet.

In the last quarter of 2019, an internal audit was conducted by the Department of Defense Inspector General (DODIG). The audit was focused on the Super Hornet fleet and was released in an official report dated November 19, 2019. The Naval Defense Logistics Agency (DLA) identified the requirement of spare parts, including its best estimation of quantities. However, it was unable to obtain them and fill the back orders. In the report, the Inspector General warned that back orders and cannibalization efforts could very well prevent the Navy from meeting sudden unexpected increases in operational mission readiness requirements in the near future.

Another Block 53 Rhino assigned to VFA-122 is seen here on the NAS Lemoore flight line. The aircraft, built under construction number 1516/F018, ordered in FY1998 and delivered to the Navy in September 2000, is seen here on the "crippled" line at NAS Lemoore in March 2014. During this time, spare parts from aircraft assigned to the Fleet Replacement Squadrons (FRS) were used to keep the operational aircraft in combat capable condition. During a later stage, aircraft assigned to the FRSs were traded with the non-combat capable aircraft of the operational squadrons.

The estimations concerning the actual mission capable Super Hornets varied from approximately two-thirds to one-half of the 546-strong Super Hornet fleet which were operational in 2018. As a result, the Navy cannibalized grounded aircraft for spare parts to such an extent that the Marine Corps even had to dismantle aircraft on display in museums in order to obtain all the necessary parts. All of this was undertaken to avoid sending requests for parts up the chain of command.

Besides the actual aircraft, the engines were also dismantled, further decreasing the inventory and number of operational aircraft. To chart the frequency of cannibalization, the Inspector General related the number of cannibalization jobs per every 100 operational flights, stating that "from October 2016 through December 2018, for the E and F models of the Super Hornet the average cannibalization rate was about 10 percent of operational flights for the E model and about 12 percent of operational flights for the F model." One of the conclusions in the Inspector General's report was that this situation was non-sustainable, and the Navy was confronted with not achieving their aircraft availability key performance indicator by the Government Accountability Office.

With a large part of the Pentagon's available funds being assigned to the acquisition of new aircraft, like the F-35 Lightning II and other new designed systems, maintaining the existing aircraft and systems received a lower-than-expected priority in the assignment of funds. The fifth generation F-35 is the most expensive aircraft purchase in the history of the Navy, and it had to deal with overspends in budget, delays, and shortages in the specified performance of the aircraft. Expecting the F-35 deliveries, the Navy canceled several contracts to continue acquiring spare parts for the Super Hornets over the past two decades. With the delay in the integration of the F-35, however, the Navy is facing the consequences of that decision.

The five critical spare parts required to maintain the operational readiness of the Super Hornet were identified. These parts were the center cockpit display, the primary targeting sensor, the communication antenna, the actuator for the tail rudder, and the electrical generator. The DODIG's

The Super Hornets that were not combat capable were either transferred to the FRS or put in short-term storage. Some of the aircraft were temporary cannibalized to keep the remaining aircraft in an operational state. The readiness recovery program ensured that the scarce spare parts were acquired and all aircraft were repaired, ready to return to active service.

report mentioned several specific causes contributing to the back orders, including obsolete materials that are no longer manufactured or available for purchase, the delivery times of manufactured spare parts, the delays in repairs, and the lack of technical data used in producing or repairing spare parts.

Alternative methods to acquire the obsolete parts, like the center cockpit display and the communication antennas, have been developed but were pending the process of approvals for the management of change during 2020. The report also stated that the original equipment manufacturer (OEM), Boeing, was unable to provide spare communication antennas for the aircraft. The Navy could, conceivably, manufacture replacements by itself, or have found a second supplier for the parts, but the Navy does not own the technical drawings for the parts, which meant this path could not be pursued.

Navy officials stated they had progressed the process to approve a new type of glass for a display replacement. There was only one vendor able to make the Super Hornet's communication antenna, however, and it experienced delays in getting the production line running, leaving DLA without a contract in place to obtain the antennas for a 13-month period.

The Navy was taking steps to rectify the obsolete parts situation with the highest priority. Nevertheless, there were still hurdles to tackle, including the lack of information sharing between the OEM and the Navy and its prospective new contractors. The Navy also faced issues with contractors either not responding to data requests or charging prohibitively expensive fees to use the data, further hampering the efforts to develop in-house repair capabilities.

Furthermore, the DODIG report stated that if the Navy had performed the necessary logistic assessments in the previous two decades, it would have been able to anticipate the shortages in spare parts and proactively approach the original manufacturer to find solutions for the parts that were critical and, in some instances, obsolete. The logistic assessments, which should have taken place every five years, were not performed between 2000 and 2018.

The DODIG report continued, "the F/A-18 E/F Program Office, referred to as PMA-265, stated that a lack of sustainment funding contributed to the difficulties with acquiring spare parts. The Chief of the Naval Operations Office stated that PMA-265 received reduced funding because PMA-265 officials had under-executed its budget and Naval Aviation sustainment budgets were all reduced." During that period, the program office requested US$193–311m, but it received US$85–136m. The Chief of Naval Operations officials explained that all budgets were reduced and that, during that time, the sustainment funding for Naval Aviation programs was not the priority with the limited funds available.

Starting in late 2015, VFA-113 transitioned aircraft and acquired a brand-new set of 12 factory fresh Lot 36 F/A-18E Super Hornets acquired in FY2012.

Above: Although VFA-146 is a F/A-18E squadron, BuNo 166666 was noted at NAS Fallon in September 2019 in full VFA-146 markings.

Right: On July 21, 1989, VA-146 was redesignated VFA-146, and the squadron received its first F/A-18C Hornet on November 18, 1989. After the squadron returned from its CVW-11 deployment onboard CVN-68 USS *Nimitz* in April 2013, VFA-146 underwent an extensive maintenance phase to transfer 14 Lot 10 F/A-18C Hornets to other squadrons and AMARG.

The commander aircraft of VFA-137 "Kestrels" at the NAS Lemoore flight line in June 2017 when VFA-137 was still assigned to Carrier Air Wing 2.

Above: The Legacy Hornets have now been withdrawn from use from all the operational Strike Fighter Squadrons within the Navy. During 2020, the Navy also stated its intention to replace the last F/A-18C models assigned to NAWDC and the adversary squadrons with Super Hornets.

Left: In 2019 East Coast squadron VFA-31 "Tomcatters" was assigned to Carrier Air Wing 11.

Below: Equal to VFA-31 "Tomcatters," VFA-87 "Golden Warriors" was assigned to Carrier Air Wing 11.

Chapter 9
Naval Squadron Reforms

The current mission capable status of the Super Hornet fleet, and the introduction of the first fifth-generation F-35C fighters with VFA-147 "Argonauts," led to several changes in carrier air wing assignments for the Hornet and Growler squadrons. In the past few years, a modest number of Super Hornets that were assigned to the FRSs VFA-106 "Gladiators" and VFA-122 "Flying Eagles" have been passed on to the operational squadrons, with the intent to keep the squadrons fully fitted with mission capable aircraft.

As a result, some of the operational squadrons been reassigned to different air wings to be as adaptive as possible to deal with the current situation and further pave the road for the implementation of the F-35C within the operational squadrons.

An overview of the situation of the operational Strike Fighter Squadrons, including the adversary squadrons operating the Legacy Hornets, was presented at the end of 2020.

Squadron	Aircraft	Status	Fleet	Emblem
VFA-2 Strike Fighter Squadron 2 "Bounty Hunters"	F/A-18F	ACTIVE	Pacific Fleet	
VFA-11 Strike Fighter Squadron 11 "Red Rippers"	F/A-18F	ACTIVE	Atlantic Fleet	
VFA-14 Strike Fighter Squadron 14 "Tophatters"	F/A-18E	ACTIVE	Pacific Fleet	
VFA-15 Strike Fighter Squadron 15 "Valions"	F/A-18E	Decommissioned on May 31, 2017	Atlantic Fleet	
VFA-22 Strike Fighter Squadron 22 "Fighting Redcocks"	F/A-18F	ACTIVE	Pacific Fleet	
VFA-25 Strike Fighter Squadron 25 "Fist of the Fleet"	F/A-18E	ACTIVE	Pacific Fleet	
VFA-27 Strike Fighter Squadron 27 "Chargers/Royal Maces"	F/A-18E	ACTIVE	Pacific Fleet	
VFA-31 Strike Fighter Squadron 31 "Tomcatters"	F/A-18F	ACTIVE	Atlantic Fleet	
VFA-32 Strike Fighter Squadron 32 "Swordsmen"	F/A-18F	ACTIVE	Atlantic Fleet	

Squadron	Aircraft	Status	Fleet	Emblem
VFA-34 Strike Fighter Squadron 34 "Blue Blasters"	F/A-18E	ACTIVE	Atlantic Fleet	
VFA-37 Strike Fighter Squadron 37 "Ragin' Bulls"	F/A-18E	ACTIVE	Atlantic Fleet	
VFA-41 Strike Fighter Squadron 41 "Black Aces"	F/A-18F	ACTIVE	Pacific Fleet	
VFA-81 Strike Fighter Squadron 81 "Sunliners"	F/A-18E	ACTIVE	Atlantic Fleet	
VFA-82 Strike Fighter Squadron 82 "Marauders"	F/A-18E	Decommissioned on September 30, 2005	Atlantic Fleet	
VFA-83 Strike Fighter Squadron 83 "Rampagers"	F/A-18E	ACTIVE	Atlantic Fleet	
VFA-86 Strike Fighter Squadron 86 "Sidewinders"	F/A-18E	ACTIVE	Pacific Fleet	
VFA-87 Strike Fighter Squadron 87 "Golden Warriors"	F/A-18E	ACTIVE	Atlantic Fleet	
VFA-94 Strike Fighter Squadron 94 "Mighty Shrikes"	F/A-18F	ACTIVE	Pacific Fleet	
VFA-97 Strike Fighter Squadron 97 "Warhawks"	F-35C	ACTIVE	Pacific Fleet	
VFA-101 Strike Fighter Squadron 101 "Grim Reapers"	F-35C	Decommissioned on May 23, 2019	Atlantic Fleet	
VFA-102 Strike Fighter Squadron 102 "Diamondbacks"	F/A-18F	ACTIVE	Pacific Fleet	
VFA-103 Strike Fighter Squadron 103 "Jolly Rogers"	F/A-18F	ACTIVE	Atlantic Fleet	

Squadron	Aircraft	Status	Fleet	Emblem
VFA-105 Strike Fighter Squadron 105 "Gunslingers"	F/A-18E	ACTIVE	Atlantic Fleet	
VFA-106 Strike Fighter Squadron 106 "Gladiators"	F/A-18E/F	ACTIVE	Atlantic Fleet	
VFA-113 Strike Fighter Squadron 113 "Stingers"	F/A-18E	ACTIVE	Pacific Fleet	
VFA-115 Strike Fighter Squadron 115 "Eagles"	F/A-18E	ACTIVE	Pacific Fleet	
VFA-122 Strike Fighter Squadron 122 "Flying Eagles"	F/A-18E/F	ACTIVE	Pacific Fleet	
VFA-125 Strike Fighter Squadron 125 "Rough Raiders"	F-35C	ACTIVE	Pacific Fleet	
VFA-127 Strike Fighter Squadron 127 "Desert Bogeys"	F/A-18C	Decommissioned on March 23, 1996	Pacific Fleet	
VFA-131 Strike Fighter Squadron 131 "Wildcats"	F/A-18E	ACTIVE	Atlantic Fleet	
VFA-132 Strike Fighter Squadron 132 "Privateers"	F/A-18E	Decommissioned on June 1, 1992	Atlantic Fleet	
VFA-136 Strike Fighter Squadron 136 "Knighthawks"	F/A-18E	ACTIVE	Pacific Fleet	
VFA-137 Strike Fighter Squadron 137 "Kestrels"	F/A-18E	ACTIVE	Pacific Fleet	
VFA-143 Strike Fighter Squadron 143 "Pukin' Dogs"	F/A-18E	ACTIVE	Atlantic Fleet	

Squadron	Aircraft	Status	Fleet	Emblem
VFA-146 Strike Fighter Squadron 146 "Blue Diamonds"	F/A-18E	ACTIVE	Atlantic Fleet	
VFA-147 Strike Fighter Squadron 147 "Argonauts"	F-35C	ACTIVE	Pacific Fleet	
VFA-151 Strike Fighter Squadron 151 "Vigilantes"	F/A-18E	ACTIVE	Pacific Fleet	
VFA-154 Strike Fighter Squadron 154 "Black Knights"	F/A-18F	ACTIVE	Pacific Fleet	
VFA-192 Strike Fighter Squadron 192 "Golden Dragons"	F/A-18E	ACTIVE	Pacific Fleet	
VFA-195 Strike Fighter Squadron 195 "Dambusters"	F/A-18E	ACTIVE	Pacific Fleet	
VFA-201 Strike Fighter Squadron 201 "Hunters"	F/A-18A	Decommissioned on June 30, 2007	Reserve	
VFA-203 Strike Fighter Squadron 203 "Blue Dolphins"	F/A-18C	Decommissioned on June 30, 2004	Reserve	
VFA-204 Strike Fighter Squadron 204 "River Rattlers"	F/A-18C	ACTIVE	Reserve	
VFA-211 Strike Fighter Squadron 211 "Fighting Checkmates"	F/A-18F	ACTIVE	Atlantic Fleet	
VFA-213 Strike Fighter Squadron 213 "Black Lions"	F/A-18F	ACTIVE	Atlantic Fleet	
VFA-303 Strike Fighter Squadron 303 "Golden Hawks"	F/A-18A	Decommissioned on December 31, 1994	Reserve	
VFA-305 Strike Fighter Squadron 305 "Lobos"	F/A-18A	Decommissioned on December 31, 1994	Reserve	

In a more recent change, VFA-97 "Warhawks" passed on its aircraft to VFA-137 "Kestrels." The aircraft previously assigned to VFA-137 were redistributed over the remaining squadrons. VFA-137 "Kestrels" was transferred from CVW-2 to CVW-17, exchanging its modex from NE-2xx to NA-3xx.

Carrier Air Wing 17 saw additional changes as well. VFA-94 "Mighty Shrikes" changed its modex from NA-4xx to NA-2xx. VFA-97 "Warhawks," previously assigned modex NA-3xx, left CVW-17 and was assigned a slightly different modex, NG-xx. With only a few Super Hornets remaining, the squadron has taken on an adversary role and its aircraft were painted in an adversary color scheme. VFA-113 "Stingers" transferred from CVW-17 to CVW-2 and is currently assigned modex NE-2xx.

VFA-147 "Argonauts" is currently assigned to CVW-2 as the first Naval F-35 squadron to reach operational capability status. VFA-192 "Golden Dragons" previously assigned modex NE-3xx is now presenting modex NE-2xx.

Both VFA-31 "Tomcatters" and VFA-87 "Golden Warriors" were assigned to CVW-11 after moving from CVW-8. Earlier in 2017, VFA-86 "Sidewinders" transferred from CVW-3 to CVW-7 and, in 2018, VFA-25 "Fist of the Fleet" transferred from CVW-9 to CVW-7. The Super Hornet inventory was subjected to the squadron reforms and is currently organized according to the table on p. 69–72.

Moving On

The Super Hornet conversion program was completed in February 2019, with VFA-37 "Bulls" and VFA-34 "Blue Blasters" being the last to make the change. The remaining Legacy Hornets were assigned to the adversary squadrons, the NAWDC, and the Blue Angels. These Legacy Hornets will gradually also be withdrawn from use and replaced by the Super Hornet.

In February 2020, the first Super Hornet submitted to the SLM program was delivered back to the US Navy. During this 18-month program, the service lifetime of the Super Hornet was extended from 6,000 to 7,500 flight hours, an increase of 25 percent. Fifteen Super Hornets were in the SLM process, with a second aircraft returned in February, and a third in April 2020. Five aircraft were planned for delivery in 2020.

In March 2019, Boeing was awarded a contract for the delivery of 61 F/A-18E and 17 F/A-18F Super Hornet Block III aircraft. The delivery of this initial batch is scheduled between FY2020–22. All 78 Super Hornets covered by this contract were Block III aircraft, which possess an increased mission range and can carry additional weapons on an increased sustainable airframe, which is expected to last 10,000 operational flight hours. This is 4,000 hours more than the Block I and Block II aircraft, equivalent to approximately an additional decade of lifetime use. In late 2020, a borders modification program commenced to further expand the Super Hornets' service life to 10,000 flight hours.

VFA-137 transferred from Carrier Air Wing 2 to Carrier Air Wing 17 in 2019. Captured here on the NAS Lemoore flight line in June 2017, the aircraft were still assigned to Carrier Air Wing 2, presenting their NE modex.

In February 2020, however, the US Navy stated it wanted to limit production of the F/A-18E/F Super Hornets in order to allocate resources to the development of the Next Generation Air Dominance (NGAD) carrier-based fighter program, as stated in the US Navy FY2020 budget request. As such, the contract for an additional 24 Super Hornets from Boeing in 2021 would be the last one on the order books for the US Navy under that plan.

The Navy's funding planned for a subsequent multi-year plan to acquire 36 additional Super Hornets between 2022 and 2024 to be reassigned to the "accelerated development of NGAD, previously known as the F/A-XX program, and other strategic aviation investments." The NGAD program was initiated to replace the payload capacity of the Super Hornets on carrier decks, since the incoming F-35C Lightning II brought a stealth fighter to the air wing. The program had a lengthy specification phase during the past decade as the Navy struggled with progressive insights in shaping the future of the carrier air wing.

The Navy stated that the decision to cease further Super Hornet procurement after FY2021 ensured the carrier air wing could maintain capable strike fighter capacity to face the most stressing threats until at least 2030. During the past five years, the US Navy has been widely criticized for not modernizing its carrier air wings to keep up with the growing threat of longer-range guided missiles that can put the fleet at risk.

A study released in 2020 stated that, in order for carrier air wings to be effective in possible future major conflicts, it would need to develop aircraft that could operate consistently at ranges of up to 1,000 nautical miles from the carrier. That is twice the current effective combat range of an F-35C.

With modernization programs implemented to further extend the service life of existing Super Hornets and Growlers, maintenance became a vital effort to keep the fleet operational and combat capable. By continuing to optimize maintenance processes, procedures, and work instructions, the Navy has the unique opportunity to keep on top of things and keep the key performance indicators "in the green."

On April 30, 2020, the final Block II Super Hornet — BuNo 169746, construction number E322 — was completed. The aircraft was delivered to VFA-34 "Blue Blasters" on April 17, 2020. With this final delivery of Block II Super Hornets, the Navy would now direct its focus to the Block III deliveries.

The new Block III configuration has an increased airframe life of 10,000 hours. The Block III further comprised five major design features: an advanced cockpit system that combined legacy displays into a single glass touchscreen for easier use; additional conformal fuel tanks that added about 3,500lb of fuel-carrying capacity and increased the range of the jet; an advanced radar cross-section improvement that made the jets harder to track by increasingly sophisticated enemy systems; an advanced networking infrastructure that included a distributed targeting network processor to add computing power and process data faster to aid the pilot in decision-making; and an infrared search and track

This F/A-18C Block 35 Hornet joined NAWDC after VFA-15 was disbanded. In February 2016, plans were announced to deactivate VFA-15 in FY2017. The deactivation ceremony took place on May 31, 2017, and the squadron was deactivated on the same day. The aircraft was transferred to NAWDC and is currently painted in a brown and white scheme, also referred to as "the antelope."

system aimed at fifth-generation competitors, scanning the horizon for radar-evading adversaries, picking up the infrared heat created by their engines.

The initial ordered batch of 24 Block III deliveries commenced in the fall of 2020, with the majority delivered in 2021. The first two Block III test jets, one F/A-18E and one F/A-18F, made their initial test flights on May 14, 2020, and were scheduled to be delivered by the end of May to the Test and Evaluation Squadrons at NAS Patuxent River and NAW China Lake.

Additionally, Boeing's production line capability is being used for the Block III SLM conversions, which will start delivering the first converted aircraft in 2023 and will continue through mid-2030.

While the Navy has accepted the delivery of its first two Block III Super Hornets to begin testing, the pressure is on to decide, within a short-term period, what its path forward will be, with either continuing to buy new F/A-18s from Boeing or focusing on developing a next-generation aircraft. The decision to cease the Super Hornet production line opened the possibility of freeing up the Boeing production line and workforce to focus on the SLM program. This would retain the desired balance of Super Hornets versus F-35 Lightnings in the carrier air wing and would also deliver greater capability and more service life on the converted jets.

Earlier in 2015, the Navy announced its intent to end Super Hornet purchases but almost immediately reversed that decision as a result of a fighter shortfall, due to using up flight hours faster than planned. The Navy reserved its budget to acquire new Super Hornets in FY2016–17, but then

Above: VFA-192 returned from NAF Atsugi in 2009 and was transferred from CVW-5 to CVW-9. In March 2014, the "Golden Dragon" Squadron was transferred to CVW-2 and currently still resides there.

Right: By 2016, the Naval Command limited the colorful markings on the commander aircraft. This image presents the VFA-22 "Redcocks" commander aircraft without any special markings in September 2018.

canceled the program in 2018. It later reversed that decision after acknowledging an ongoing fighter shortfall that needed to be addressed. This is the first time the Navy has tried to cancel the Super Hornet production line since 2017.

The FY2020 plan included the acquisition of 148 aircraft. The request included:

- Twenty F-35Cs, a four-aircraft increase compared to 2019's plan
- Ten F-35Bs for the USMC, a ten-aircraft decrease compared to 2019
- Twenty-four additional F/A-18E-F Super Hornets
- Four E-2D Advanced Hawkeye AEW aircraft
- Six P-8A maritime surveillance aircraft, a three-aircraft decrease from 2019
- Three KC-130J cargo and refueling aircraft
- An additional 22 F-5E/F light supersonic fighters from Switzerland to serve as adversary aircraft during training
- Six CH-53K heavy-lift helicopters for the Marine Corps, three fewer compared to 2019
- Ten CMV-22B Ospreys, which will replace the C-2A as the carrier onboard delivery aircraft
- Thirty-two Advanced Helicopter Training Systems, an increase of five compared to 2019
- Six VH-92A presidential helicopters
- Two MQ-4C Triton unmanned maritime surveillance aircraft, a decrease of one compared to 2019's plan
- Three MQ-9A Reaper unmanned aircraft for the Marine Corps to train its unmanned aerial systems operators to work with large Group 4/5 UAVs

The spending plan shows further decreases to aircraft procurement compared to previous years. The F-35B program for the Marines was cut by ten aircraft in 2020, five in 2021, three in 2022, and one in 2023. The Navy's Super Hornet acquisition program is steady with plans in 2020 and 2021, but it will be reduced by nine in 2022 and five in 2023. The F-35C procurement plan totals remain steady from 2020 through 2023, but eight aircraft are shifted from 2021 to later years.

The cuts to the aircraft procurement over the Fiscal Year Development Plan were partly due to trying to find the correct balance of tactical aircraft and changes the Marine Corps made to its squadron transition plan between the F-35B and F-35C variants.

VFA-147 operated Lot 26 F/A-18E Hornets. BuNo 166447 modex NH-212 is seen here maneuvering through Rainbow Canyon, also referred to as Star Wars Canyon or Jedi Transition.

Naval Squadron Reforms

In October 2009, VFA-154 transitioned to the new F/A-18F Block II Lot 30/31A AN/APG-79 AESA radar Rhino. In 2010 the squadron relocated from Carrier Air Wing 9 to Carrier Air Wing 14 aboard CVN-76 USS *Ronald Reagan*.

In January 2012, after returning from its Unit Deployment Progam in Japan, VFA-94 "Mighty Shrikes" returned to NAS Lemoore. However, it was not assigned to one of the West Coast air wings until around August 2012, as it temporarily took sister squadron VFA-25's place within CVW-17.

Chapter 10

Electronic Attack Squadron Developments

The Boeing EA-18G Growler was designed in the early 2000s, developed to overtake the Electronic Warfare Aircraft role from the Grumman EA-6B Prowler, further integrating the multi-role task within the standardized F/A-18 Hornet platform. By integrating the Electronic Attack role into the Hornet and developing the EA-18G based on the F/A-18F Block II design, the Navy aimed to utilize the state-of-the-art electronic warfare hardware and jamming software to blind opposing air defenses.

A new demonstration aircraft based on the F/A-18F was first flown in November 2001. The Navy signed a development contract with Boeing in December 2003 for further development, which commenced in 2004. Two evaluation aircraft, registered as the EA-1 and EA-2, were then constructed for the various testing phases to follow. First flight of an EA-18G Growler was recorded on August 15, 2006, and this was subsequently followed by delivery of the first production-quality Growler in 2007. Fleet Readiness Squadron VAQ-129 of NAS Whidbey Island, Washington, received the Growler on June 3, 2008. Sea trials were successfully completed in August 2008 from the deck of the aircraft carrier CVN-69 USS *Dwight D. Eisenhower*. Initial Operational Test and Evaluation wrapped up in May 2009 and formal introduction of the system for operational status within the Navy inventory commenced on September 22, 2009. Full-rate production was ordered by the government in November 2009, and the first batch of aircraft was delivered by the end of 2010.

On September 28, 2010, Boeing received a contract for 66 Super Hornets and a further 58 Growlers from the Navy. On May 5, 2014, the 100th EA-18G was delivered to NAS Whidbey Island. The final batches of Growlers ordered were Lot 39 in FY2015 and Lot 40 in FY2016. Lot 39 would include the delivery of 15 Growlers, BuNos 169206–169220, and Lot 40 would include the delivery of seven Growlers, BuNos 169400–169406. These two last batches left the production line at St. Louis between 2019 and 2020.

The EA-18G Growler integrated the latest state-of-the-art electronic attack technology, including the ALQ-218 receiver, ALQ-99 jamming pods, communication countermeasures, and satellite communications. The AN/ALQ-249, the Next Generation Jammer Pod, is in final development, with IOC expected in FY2022, and will be the successor for the long serving ALQ-99 pods. Along with the electronic attack suite, the Growler also features the APG-79 AESA radar.

In 2015, VAQ-129 successfully completed the transition of all fleet squadrons from the EA-6B Prowler to the Growler. BuNo 158810 arrived at NAS Fallon in September 2013 to be preserved in the NAS Fallon Air Park.

Four Navy expeditionary VAQ squadrons uniquely support United Stated Air Force and Navy shore-based operations. All EA-18G squadrons are stationed at NAS Whidbey Island, with the exception of one squadron, VAQ-141 "Shadowhawks," assigned to Carrier Air Wing 5, the forward deployed Naval Force, based at MCAS Iwakuni in Japan.

Growler Modifications

In early 2020, the Navy awarded Boeing initial funding to begin studying what kind of technologies could be incorporated into a "Block II Growler." The Navy was interested in retrofitting a number of its EA-18G Growlers during the mid-2020s. As of March 2021, the Block II was in development and included the improvement of the Growler's electronic attack sensors. It was considering enhancements to Northrop Grumman's ALQ-218 sensor system, which was used by the Growler for radar warning, electronic support measures, and electronic intelligence. The upgrade also included the addition of an adaptive and distributed processing system, enabling the EA-18 Growler computers to quickly digest and process threat information.

The Block II upgrades will also contain some capabilities that Boeing has already developed for the latest Block III iteration of the Super Hornet, such as low-drag conformal fuel tanks. The company is also assessing whether to further increase the Growler's 7,500-hour service life as part of the retrofit process.

Above left: In May 2014, VAQ-131 completed its conversion to the EA-18G Growler, trading in its EA-6B Prowlers. The EA-18G expanded the squadron's capabilities to enable more effective prosecution of radar and Surface-to-Air Missile (SAM) sites in an Integrated Air Defense System (IADS), both through air-to-ground weapon employment and precision electronic attack, the latter being the Growler's niche capability. BuNo 163884 was transferred to 309th AMARG on March 4, 2014.

Above right: An EA-18G proceeds to the runway for another mission during the Carrier Air Wing 7 work-up training at NAS Fallon in October 2018.

Below: BuNo 168371, assigned to VAQ-140, is a Lot 34 EA-18G Growler acquired in FY2010. Upon delivery in 2012, the Growler was initially assigned to VAQ-129 and transferred to VAQ-140 in 2014.

Above left: After completing its 2010 deployment, VAQ-139 "Cougars" transitioned from the EA-6B Prowler to the EA-18 Growler. Upon completing the transition in 2012, the "Cougars" began workups for its inaugural EA-18G deployment with Carrier Air Wing 17.

Above right: VAQ-139 "Cougars" received a batch of Lot 33 EA-18G Growlers in 2011, trading in its EA-6B Prowlers which it has been operating from 1983 onward.

Left: Electronic Attack Squadron 142, or VAQ-142, also referred to as "The Gray Wolves," is an EA-18G Growler squadron of NAS Whidbey Island. It is attached to CVW-11.

Below: NAWDC operates four EA-18G Growlers. BuNo 168942 modex 501 is a Lot 37 EA-18G acquired in FY2013 delivered to NAWDC on January 29, 2015. The Growler was delivered to the US Navy on January 29, 2015, and was delivered factory fresh to NAWDC at NAS Fallon in March 2015.

Chapter 11
Patrol Squadron Developments

The Patrol Squadrons continued to fulfil an important role in Early Warning capability. Although the now aging P-3 Orion and P-8 Poseidon were land-based aircraft unable to land on an aircraft carrier, they were a vital asset to relay information to the carrier strike group. Both platforms could exchange information with the E-2C and E-2D Hawkeye, and, to a lesser extent, the EA-18G Growler.

The P-3C subtype of the P-3 Orion was the last of the surviving Orions in the fleet. VP-69 "Totems," subordinated to COMRESPATWING, was the final remaining squadron at NAS Whidbey Island operating the P-3C BMUP+ (Block Modification Upgrade Program).

The Lockheed P-3 Orion was introduced within the Naval Patrol Squadrons in 1962. Patrol Squadron 8 (VP-8) at NAS Patuxent River was the first operational squadron to receive the P3V-1 Orion, later designated P-3A by the Navy as BuNo 149671, on August 13, 1962. By the end of October 1962, VP-8 reached operational status, equipped with 12 P-3A Orions.

On March 22, 1990, VP-64 flew the last operational United States Navy P-3A mission. In the meantime, VP-22 had completed the last P-3B frontline mission on September 11, 1990. From that moment on, the P-3B was only in use with reserve squadrons. Late in 1987, the P-3C-III was introduced in the Naval Reserve Force with VP-62 being the first reserve squadron to receive factory fresh Orions. The very final P-3B mission was flown by VP-93 and, since October 1994, all Navy Patrol Squadrons were operating P-3C versions. Sixty-eight Orions were modified for anti-surface warfare (ASuW) in the Anti-Surface Warfare Improvement Program. In addition, 30 aircraft have been modified to carry and launch Maverick missiles.

After a long selection process, on June 4, 2004, the USN decided that the P-3C Orions would be replaced by the maritime patrol version of the Boeing 737-800ERX. This decision was announced ten days later, on June 14, 2004. A total number of 109 Boeing P-8As were purchased, with the first delivery to VP-30 in 2013. On August 2, 2004, the Embraer ERJ-145 was selected as the replacement for the EP-3E fleet.

The US Navy's 2021 budget proposal will apparently request no new money to purchase more P-8As, despite a growing undersea threat and a shortfall in aircraft designed to cope with that threat. Congressional appropriators asked the Navy in December 2019 how it would replace the P-3C Orions in the two Navy Reserve squadrons, which must retire in the near future, if production of the P-8 is prematurely terminated.

The Navy continued to deploy the Lockheed P-3 Orion at the start of the 2000s, which remained in high demand across a range of missions including anti-submarine warfare, anti-surface warfare, and time critical intelligence, surveillance, and reconnaissance. Up until 2001, 99 Orions were scheduled to go through the Sustained Readiness Program to increase their technical lifetime to 38 years, but after completion of 13 aircraft, the program was terminated because the contractor, Raytheon E-Systems, was overrunning the budget and had encountered numerous technical problems. Another 19 aircraft went through a simple program, which only extended the airframe lifetime four years. The Navy investigated the possibility of funding a SLEP, which was planned for FY2002.

The P-3C sustainment program kept the aging aircraft operational as the Navy further integrated the P-8A Poseidon into the Patrol Squadrons starting in 2013. The P-8A was a long-range multi-mission maritime patrol aircraft capable of broad-area, maritime, and littoral operations. The P-8A combined superior performance and reliability with an advanced mission system that ensured maximum interoperability in the battle space.

The P-8A operated very differently from the P-3, but the fundamentals of being a pilot remained the same. Compared to the P-3C Orion, the aircraft had additional technological features integrated and enabled the crew to access significant amounts of information. Knowing what information was important and relevant at any given moment still took practice and training. Automation made the aircraft operate more safely, but it was limited by the understanding and ability of the person managing the automation to make safe and timely decisions.

The P-8A possessed an active multi-static and passive acoustic sensor system, inverse synthetic aperture radar, new electronic support measures system, new electro-optical/infrared sensor, and a digital magnetic anomaly detector.

It fit a total of nine crewmembers, including a dual-pilot cockpit and room for five mission crew, plus a relief pilot and in-flight technician's cockpit. The P-8A had workstations with universal multi-function displays and ready accommodation for additional workstations and workload sharing. The Poseidon was armed with an internal five-station weapons bay, four wing pylons and two centerline pylons, all supported by digital stores management allowing for carriage of joint missiles, torpedoes, and mines. Boeing was awarded the contract to develop the P-8A on June 14, 2004. The P-8A was a derivative of a modified Boeing 737-800ERX airliner, bringing together a reliable airframe and high-bypass turbo fan jet engine with a fully connected, state-of-the-art open architecture mission system.

Coupled with next-generation sensors, the P-8A was intended to improve anti-submarine and anti-surface warfare capabilities. The P-8A program went through a preliminary design review in November 2005. The Navy planned to purchase 108 production P-8As. The first aircraft was scheduled to be delivered for flight test in 2009, with IOC planned for 2013. The P-8A was militarized with maritime weapons, a modern open mission system architecture, and commercial-like support for affordability. The aircraft was modified to include a bomb bay and pylons for weapons and could carry 129 sonobuoys. The aircraft was also fitted with an in-flight refueling system. With more than 180,000 flight hours to date, P-8 variants – the P-8A Poseidon and the P-8I – patrol the globe performing anti-submarine and anti-surface warfare, intelligence, surveillance and reconnaissance, humanitarian missions, and search and rescue missions.

In May 2020, Boeing delivered the 100th P-8A aircraft. This was the 94th mission-capable aircraft to enter the US Navy fleet, with the remaining six jets used as Engineering Manufacturing Development Test aircraft. Patrol Squadron 40 (VP-40), the "Fighting Marlins," completed the final transition on May 14, 2020, with the service announced on May 28. The squadron started the transition in November 2019.

VP-10 traded the P-3C Orion for the factory new P-8A Poseidons in March 2015, its first transition in 50 years. In 2018, VP-10 deployed to the United States Sixth Fleet Area of Responsibility, flying nearly 5,000 hours while conducting ASW, ISR, CSG support, Theatre Security and Cooperation, and numerous NATO and allied exercises in over a dozen detachments to nine countries. VP-10 was awarded the 2018 Battle Effectiveness Award.

VP-4 transferred to the P-8A Poseidon in October 2016. Seen here landing on NAS North Island is BuNo 162775 in 2015.

Chapter 12
Carrier Airborne Early Warning Squadron Developments

Expanding the Eye of the Fleet

The Grumman E-2 Hawkeye proved to be a very reliable Early Warning platform for the United States Navy over the past decades. The current versions of the Hawkeye, the E-2C and the E-2C-2000, became operational in 1973 and surpassed one million flight hours in August 2004. The aircraft underwent several upgrades to its active and passive sensors, engines, and propellers. The latest E-2C variant, the Hawkeye 2000, with its new mission computer, improved radar displays and Cooperative Engagement Capability, combined with the shipboard Aegis weapon system, forms the cornerstone of today's sea-based Integrated Air and Missile Defense.

The Hawkeye's Airborne Tactical Data System, equipped with auto-detection radar, airborne computers, and a memory and data link system, was directly linked to the Naval Tactical Data System, which created an overall picture of the tactical situation within the area of operation. The Hawkeye's 24ft rotating radar dish rotated at a rate of six rotations per minute (rpm) and could gather any required information. The five-man crew consisted of two pilots and three equipment operators. The equipment operators monitored a large number of contacts at any given time, directing strike aircraft to assigned targets, in all weather conditions, while maintaining a watch for hostile forces within the long range of their radar. Working as a team, the Hawkeye provided the fleet with an early warning umbrella, capable of directing air defenses against any adversary.

The E-2C and E-2C-2000 were equipped with radar capability, detecting targets anywhere within a 3m cubic mile surveillance envelope while simultaneously monitoring maritime traffic. Each Hawkeye also performed all-weather patrols, automatically and simultaneously tracked more than 600 targets, and controlled more than 40 airborne intercepts.

The E-2 platform was in continuous development and, since 2018, deliveries of the E-2D were another step in enhancing capabilities of early warning and command and control aircraft. The enhanced capabilities of the E-2D redefined the use of the "Hawkeye" within the active carrier air wing deployment and the tasks appointed to the aircraft and aircrew.

Hawkeye Deployments

An E-2 Hawkeye deployment on an active aircraft carrier comprised four aircraft if the squadron was equipped with E-2C aircraft, and five aircraft if the squadron was equipped with E-2D aircraft. During deployment, the aircrew of an E-2C squadron comprised 25 persons and an E-2D squadron 35 persons. With the upgrade from E-2A to E-2C, a glass cockpit was implemented, and the aircrew increased from four to five persons, comprising two pilots and three equipment operators. With the introduction of the glass cockpit, the pilots had access to the same information as the operators in the back of the aircraft, improving their situational awareness.

Carrier Airborne Early Warning Squadron 116 (VAW-116) is a US Navy Command and Control Squadron that is part of Carrier Air Wing 17, operating the E-2C-2000 Hawkeye aircraft. VAW-116 is stationed at NAS Point Mugu under the cognizance of Commander, Airborne Command Control and Logistics Wing.

A Hawkeye squadron typically had three aircraft on the flight deck. Having the fourth or fifth aircraft on the flight deck created space issues when maneuvering around all the jets. It was more practical to keep one or two aircraft in the hangar deck to perform preventive maintenance or repairs.

During carrier deployment workup training missions at NAS Fallon, two Hawkeyes were launched prior to any mission. Although there was no real requirement to launch two aircraft, it offered a few advantages. In order to explain this, the methods of scanning need to be explained first.

The E-2C was not designed to scan small objects over a high cluttered land environment but to track larger objects over a water environment. To perform that task, the E-2C was equipped with a 24ft rotating radome, housing an APS-145, with a few remaining aircraft still equipped with the APS-139 radar.

The capability unique to the latest development was that the radar system could be operated in different modes. Firstly, the crew could rotate the dome and electronically steer the beam inside the dome. It could be compared to sitting on a rotating chair and, while rotating, your head keeps focused on a certain object. As soon as you lose sight, at a nearly 360-degree turn, a new rotation commenced, and your head was turned again. The dome was rotated like that chair, but the focus remained on the same point and, when the dome completed one rotation, the focus is picked up at the other side. It allowed the Hawkeye to send a lot more electrons downrange and receive more by means of the electronic steering.

Secondly, it was possible to lock the dome down in a fixed position. Consequently, instead of 6rpm, resulting in an update every 10–12 seconds, by not moving the dome at all and instead using the electronic steering to increase the update rate of the information within that specific area, detection and tracking capability are increased.

When the dome was locked down, however, the Hawkeye did not perform its primary mission of 360-degree surveillance, with the purpose to protect the aircraft carrier battle group. This was one of the main reasons why two Hawkeyes were launched, so one aircraft could perform a more specific search while the other performed the 360-degree search. The driving reason, however, was that the Hawkeye had a huge uptake in capability. Due to its enhanced capabilities, the Hawkeye moved from being a strike group platform to an airborne battle management centric platform. This development automatically caused additional demand which, in turn, had to be met by additional supply.

A Typical Day at the Office at Sea

A daily mission while on deployment usually started with two to three hours of mission planning. The mission planning included a look on the map to determine the geographical position of the ship, locating airfields within range to create awareness of where aircraft or ships, referred to as contacts, or threats if hostile, might be coming from and to understand the layout of the battle space in conflict situations.

After the mission planning, the crew visited all the ready rooms of the squadrons on board. During the squadron briefs, the Hawkeye crew gathered information on the daily operations. Each fighter squadron had its mission for that day and went through the air plan. This was published and discussed daily to establish who was flying with the Hawkeye on that particular mission. The Hawkeye crew also briefed the other crews on possible capability limitations they might have during that mission. This process took roughly two to three hours.

Once all the squadrons were visited and consulted, the mission brief of the E-2 crew occurred, which took approximately one hour. If there was a large force exercise planned, an additional briefing was held where all aircrews of that mission were present, taking roughly one additional hour.

Upon completion of the brief, the crew headed for the flight line to inspect, man-up and start the aircraft, which took another hour. Usually, two aircraft were launched via the first off–last down principle.

A typical peacetime mission took roughly four hours. Although it was not a requirement to start each mission with the launch of an E-2 Hawkeye, it created space on the flight deck for the remaining jets to launch. Depending on the geographical location of the carrier, for example, in an area where no threats were expected, there was no actual requirement to launch a Hawkeye. When the carrier was near a coastline, the deployment of a Hawkeye was considered necessary, whether it was a friendly or a hostile nation, to prevent anyone from flying over the carrier.

When the aircraft had safely returned to the carrier deck, another two hours of mission debrief concluded that daily mission. If the daily mission was a large force exercise, another hour was added, where a debrief was performed with all the remaining crews of that mission.

This means an operational mission for an aircrew during deployment at sea took roughly 11–12 hours a day. After performing their daily tasks, the crew had to rest and get sleep to be ready for the next cycle. A minimum of eight hours of sleep was mandatory and, at least during peacetime, the crews certainly stuck to that. During a conflict situation, 18-hour mission times were sanctioned, with only four hours of sleep in between, but, after performing these missions, a fifteen-hour resting time was required to prevent physical burnout.

A Hawkeye and its crew were also able to perform 24 hours of operation time, including preparations and de-brief time. It was not an aircraft limitation, but a human limitation. With these long mission duration times and only a 25–35-person mission crew, the required rest time in order to get enough sleep ran out fast. During a conflict this could be sanctioned, but during peacetime this was not standard operation.

Aircrew Cycles

Besides performing the daily missions and operations, a Hawkeye squadron had a dozen additional tasks and commitments. This influenced the composition of the aircrews as well. Each squadron coped with this in its own way. Due to the large variety of additional tasks, keeping one particular crew together was very difficult and a rotational system was more practical.

The additional tasks assigned to the squadron meant they had to have a daily squadron duty officer, a Landing Signals Officer, and a Carrier Air Traffic Control Center representative, also referred to as a "tower flower," who sat up at the tower in case of an emergency. Although the Air Boss was familiar

The aircraft assigned to VAW-116 all have nicknames that refer to the "King of Rock and Roll," Elvis Presley.

with most of the aircraft, he was not a subject matter expert for each type, so the squadron provided its own expert, who was able to advise on the impacts each particular emergency could have.

As a direct result from these additional tasks, during peacetime the aircrews were usually scattered. The crews trained hard on standardization, so everyone performed their tasks in the exact same manner. At the weapons school, all weapons and tactics instructors preached every day to work as standard as possible, so every crew member could operate in any aircraft in the squadron and fleet, regardless of which squadron they were previously in or when they started their deployment.

During operations *Iraqi Freedom* and *Enduring Freedom*, the E-2 crews were operating as combat crews. These crews consisted of the same five persons mainly to keep the crew on the same daily rhythm, to get sufficient sleep and rest. Although this is not driven from a teamwork perspective, as all crews are trained to perform plug-and-play missions, it helped crews get to know each other and anticipate each other. This also happened automatically as operation tempo increased.

Battle Management Role

The Hawkeye was originally designed as a single-sensor platform and operated on its own. During the last decade, the asset developed into a central information gathering and relay station and gained a battle management role. The Hawkeye had "Link-16" capabilities and could communicate and coordinate with all United States military assets and most of the coalition assets, which was the main reason why the aircraft became the key node in that tactical data link network.

While the E-2C operated from the rear within the area of operation, it had the unique capability to communicate both with the frontline forces and with the rear. With this capability, the Hawkeye eventually became the "manager" of the tactical data link system.

The gathered information could be relayed to any asset, as necessary. It was transmitted in a safe manner, using different kinds of crypto that could be configured in multiple ways. This meant that anyone could receive the data, but they were unable to use that information if they did not possess the correct crypto key.

The other AEW aircraft within the United States Navy, the P-3 Orion and the P-8 Poseidon, were also unique platforms, because they started out as surface warfare and sub-surface warfare aircraft. Due to the Poseidon's capacity to carry multiple crew members and stay airborne longer than other aircraft, they developed an immerging battle management role, which was similar to the E-2.

The P-3 and P-8, however, had different missions than the Hawkeye. This was because the latter's capabilities comprised air search and surface search radar, while the P-3 and P-8 performed surface and sub-surface searches. Comparing the P-3 or P-8 to the E-2 was not realistic. They were complimentary to the battle group, but they were not meant to be the same. The E-2 was unable to perform anti-submarine warfare tasks, with the exception that it could detect a submarine if it was on

Carrier Airborne Early Warning Squadron 117 (VAW-117) is nicknamed "The Wallbangers" (formerly "The Nighthawks"). The squadron is based in NAS Point Mugu and deploys as part of Carrier Air Wing 9 (CVW-9) aboard USS Abraham Lincoln. The squadron began conversion to the E-2D Hawkeye in November 2019.

the surface. The P-3 and P-8 dropped sonar buoys for that purpose and the E-2 could not perform that task. The E-2 did, however, have airborne control over them by means of voice controls; the E-2 also controlled the digital data links.

Both crews worked very closely together, to share as much available information between the assets as possible. For example, a P-3 or P-8 could be launched from a shore-based location and transit to the assigned area of operation. An E-2, launched later, would communicate with the anti-submarine commander of the carrier battle group that there had been possible contact in that area. The E-2 could then brief the P-3 or P-8 to concentrate on that area and find the submarine.

What made the Hawkeye unique was that it could be launched from an aircraft carrier and was assigned to the carrier strike group. The Commander, Air Group "owned" the asset, whereas the P-3 and P-8 were usually under the command of a different task force, and thus it was more difficult for the carrier strike group to get a hold of that aircraft.

Besides communicating with the ships and the fighter aircraft in the area of operation, the Hawkeye was also capable of exchanging information with other Naval Air Force platforms, like the Airborne Warning and Control System and "Wedgetail" assets via the Link-16 system.

Change Management

A conversion to a new subtype or a designed modification was a delicate process and was implemented squadron by squadron. Every new version went through a developmental test and an operational test in which experienced Hawkeye pilots went through the changes. There was an entire process the squadrons went through during the implementation stage. They looked at doctrine, training materials, and facilities. With every new capability the basic question was "what does the squadron need to change in order to bring itself up to speed?" This was prepared in detail at the Carrier Airborne Early Warning Weapons School (CAEWWS) located at NAS Fallon. There was a lot of information exchange with the developmental and operational test pilots to determine what the new capability would be used for. The NAWDC developed the tactics, techniques, and procedures that the crews used and developed a clear instruction on how to perform those new tasks. NAWDC also trained the weapons and tactics instructors, who transfer their knowledge to the squadrons. There are also type-specific wing weapons schools. For the Hawkeye, these were referred to as Airborne Command and Control and Logistics Weapons School, situated both on the East and West coasts. During conversion to a new subtype, the FRS, VAW-120, was the first squadron to receive the new aircraft and was prepared to train the future instructors.

From C to D Model

The E-2D had many advantages compared to the E-2C. In its C-model configuration, it was designed to detect large bomber-sized aircraft over water during the Cold War. With the development of the D-model, the aircraft further evolved to detect smaller objects over further ranges, including targets over high-clutter environments over land and over water.

The radar was the key. Obviously, all the communication suites were updated to the "latest and greatest" state-of-the-art technology. The unique thing about the E-2D was that it had multiple redundant systems for gathering and exchanging data. It had the capability to use VHF, UHF and SATCOM, HF, and multiple other ways to communicate if an adversary was trying to deny any of the electromagnetic spectrum. The E-2D had the ability to adapt and be flexible to what was denied or allowed by the adversary.

The E-2D was also equipped with Electronic Support Measures (ESM). This was a passive detection system. The ESM system helped the crew understand the electromagnetic spectrum that was out there. This information was linked to the battle group using Link-16, but a lot of it was also relayed vocally.

Carrier Airborne Early Warning Squadron 112 (VAW-112) is nicknamed "Golden Hawks." VAW-112 was based at NAS Point Mugu and last deployed as part of CVW-9 on board USS *John C. Stennis*. In February 2016, it was reported that VAW-112 was to be deactivated in FY2017. The squadron was actually deactivated on May 31, 2017.

Both the Air Force and Navy had assets that were specifically designed for it in the fighter configuration as well. The F-35 Lightning II and the EA-18G Growler had this capability and took care of the more complex missions. The E-2 helped to contribute to situational awareness. It was an extra piece in the intelligence puzzle, helping to provide understanding in the areas of operation.

Four Cs to five Ds

Why did the Navy operate a five-aircraft E-2D squadron compared to a four-aircraft E-2C squadron? With the introduction of the new capabilities of the E-2D, the demands of the platform were increased as well. The Hawkeye was originally designed as a carrier-based aircraft for the carrier strike group. All the joint coalition events in the past, such as operations *Iraqi Freedom*, *Inherent Resolve*, *Enduring Freedom*, and *Southern Watch*, really emphasized the need for an airborne command and control platform. However, there were not enough Air Force assets to fulfil the need. As a result, the coalition forces relied on the E-2 during all of these events. With that increased demand from the joint force, the supply had to be increased or it had to be accepted that Hawkeye squadrons could not provide support to both the naval carrier group and joint forces.

As previously discussed, E-2Cs operated in pairs most of the time. There were good reasons for that redundancy. If one aircraft had a temporary malfunctioning system, like the IFF system, the other was still operational. Likewise, if one's radar was temporarily down, the other took control until the radar came back up. More importantly, if the carrier air wing had a group of aircraft on a mission and, in the event an aircraft was in a combat role, typically it would have an entire personnel recovery taskforce coming on station when the E-2 was already there, running that mission. This flexibility created the capability to dynamically move between two missions with the two aircraft. Another advantage was the previously mentioned variety of radar modes.

Air Refueling Capability

The first Hawkeye equipped with an air refueling probe was delivered to the FRS VAW-120 on September 9, 2019. The implementation of air refueling capacity was in the developmental and operational test phase since 2017. The Navy also performed research in the development of a wet wing variant, in which the wing structure was sealed and used as a fuel tank. There were several challenges during the wet wing design process, and one issue was the weight constraint, as this option applied a great deal of additional pressure to the aircraft. The air refueling capabilities somewhat eliminated the requirement for that, but, for other nations operating the E-2 which did not have air refueling capabilities, this solution would make a lot of sense. In 2019, VAW-120 gained experience with the new capability and developed a syllabus to train the active aircrews and the next generation of pilots.

The air refueling probe was a fixed probe that stuck out of the nose right over the centerline of the cockpit and was a huge game changer. It increased the capability for time on station significantly and allowed the Hawkeye to go further from the aircraft carrier. By adding the air refueling to the enhanced radar system capabilities integrated in the E-2D, it received a much more prominent role in battle management. In this new configuration, the Hawkeye could be refueled by most of the Air Force tankers, Navy tankers (including Hornets), and most of the coalition forces' tankers.

The maximum operation time, however, including the air refueling capacity, was limited to 10 hours. The aircraft consumed oil that needed refilling and changing, and the crew endurance also reached its limitations. The flow rate of the refueling process was very high. It took approximately 6–8 minutes, once the probe was in the basket, to receive a full fuel reserve transferred from the tanker. The volume of fuel intake was dependent on where the aircraft was at each event.

The air refueling capability was only implemented on the E-2D, and only one squadron per year will make the conversion. The transition started in 2020 and is aimed to be completed around 2027–28.

Refueling in a Hawkeye was not an easy task, since it was not originally designed for an aircraft refueling mode. For this purpose, the flight control system was improved to help the crew out, but there were two propellers near the probe, and they could easily damage the probe if the process did not work out as planned. CDR Jason Fox commented that "It was the hardest thing I ever had to do and, although it might be a little tougher in a simulator than it is in actual flight since you will have a better feel with the aircraft and its performance, it took all of my experience and efforts to get the job done."

E-2D Upgrades

Equal to the E-2C, the E-2D was linked to the Naval Integrated Fire Control (NIFC), also referred to as counter air system. NIFC is a generational tracking and detection capability. Compared to the C-model, the E-2D detected contacts at a further distance in different robust environments. It allowed the E-2D to track smaller objects, like cruise missiles, in these environments, whereas the E-2C was never designed to do that and, in its current configuration, had difficulty in tracking contacts in high cluttered environments over land. The E-2C and the E-2D roughly contributed to NIFC in the same way. The information was relayed to the battle group by both types. However, the new radar provided an increase in accuracy, power, detection, and tracking of targets. With this new capability the aircraft was an integral part of NIFC.

The operational range of the E-2D compared to the E-2C was roughly the same. A Hawkeye could go 1,000 miles one way from the carrier. With the introduction of air refueling capabilities, the operational range of the Hawkeye changed, but it did not necessarily mean that the Hawkeye could operate further from the carrier. The E-2s preferred to keep the carrier in radar range, in order to defend the carrier if there was any threat. They did not have to be within carrier range, but, from a doctrinal standpoint, there was a lot of argument in the early warning community that the Hawkeyes were more a part of the airborne command and control community.

Where the history of CAEWWS was focused on early warning, the future was in enabling connecting command chains through command and control. There was a fine dividing point in the community

The all-weather E-2 Hawkeye aircraft has served as the "eyes" of the US Navy fleet for more than 30 years, and the E-2C Hawkeye 2000 possesses the most advanced Airborne Early Warning and Battle Management capabilities in service today. Continuous modifications and upgrades have kept the aircraft's mission systems current with the evolving operational environment. The next generation E-2D Advanced Hawkeye, the key airborne enabler of the US Navy's FORCEnet, began test flights in 2007.

and the E-2 community had been attempting to divorce themselves from it. The Hawkeyes developed from a sole scanner to a scanner able to fuse data, coordinate the battlefield, and make decisions rapidly in a tactical environment.

The further a Hawkeye went from the carrier, the less protection it provided, but, depending on the threat, it could be fine. For example, during Operation *Enduring Freedom*, the Hawkeyes were far away from the carrier and there was little concern about this, as the operational situation allowed it. However, whilst direct, overhead protection may lessen the further away an E-2 was. A greater distance meant it could provide an earlier warning to the battle group; it was a balancing act, and it was why operating the E-2 required unique decision making. With the increased capability, the chain towards the carrier might be broken, but the Navy fought very hard to keep the E-2 within the carrier air wing. They did not want to leave the capital ships unguarded, and that elevated sensor was important. Just how important is what they are still learning with each new mission.

All E-2C aircraft will eventually be replaced by the E-2D. A total of 75 will be purchased, and the intention is to have all the E-2Cs replaced by E-2Ds by 2027–28. The technology is that much better that there is no justification to keep the E-2C operational. The reason why the conversion is going at a seemingly slower pace is due to budgeting and the fact that the E-2Ds cannot be manufactured quickly.

VAW-113 was the first squadron to receive the E-2D on the West Coast in August 2019. It did its transition at Norfolk, for about three months, and was trained by FRS VAW-120. In the second week of September 2019, VAW-113 qualified for safe-for-flight status, which meant it was allowed to run the aircraft itself. It reestablished the "Eagle" callsign, repainted the two already received Hawkeyes and, more importantly, its maintainers turned wrenches on those aircraft without VAW-120 oversight for the first time. VAW-117 was right behind them. It started its transition over November–December. It followed the same process by going out to VAW-120 and received the same transition training. The main advantage is that VAW-113 is now able to pass on the aircraft knowledge and training, which hopefully means that squadrons will not need to train with the East Coast squadrons quite as long.

The conversion started on the East Coast for logistic reasons since that was where the test squadrons were located. They had the ability to train the FRS which was also located on the East Coast. With a pivot to the Far East, there was huge demand to get the aircraft to fly in the Pacific as soon as possible. CDR Jason Fox stated that the "aircraft were assigned first to where they were most needed but, in all reality, it comes down to the logistic chains. It took a while to get the East Coast logistic chain up and

Below left: Hawkeye 2000 is the fifth-generation production E-2C Hawkeye and incorporates significant enhancements in data management, system throughput, operator interfaces, connectivity, and situational awareness to support the Navy's evolving Theater Air and Missile Defense mission. This Hawkeye capitalizes on the previous version's Group II baseline fully integrated system, which includes the AN/APS-145 radar system, improved identification friend/foe (IFF) system, the Joint Tactical Information Distribution System (JTIDS), a global positioning system (GPS), and the Carrier Aircraft Inertial Navigational System (CAINS) II.

Below right: The Hawkeyes of VAW-115 used to be deployed to NAF Atsugi. On February 2, 2017, VAW-125 arrived at Marine Corps Air Station Iwakuni, Japan, to replace VAW-115 in CVW-5. In the summer of 2017, the squadron moved to NAS Point Mugu, where it will eventually transition to the E-2D Advanced Hawkeye. Here, it is captured landing at NAF Atsugi just before its relocation to NAS Point Mugu, with the NF code already removed.

running and when it was established, we took some of that logistic chain and put it over at the West Coast. The Navy is kind of distributing their new capability as well as they can."

Future Developments

There had been many discussions and developments into Unmanned Aircraft Systems (UAS). The future for both manned and unmanned variants is interesting. However, the *Joint Warfare of the Armed Forces of the United States* document stated that the chain-of-command communication should be kept "short and simple, so that it is clear who is in charge and of what." An unmanned vehicle that was controlled by someone on board a ship had a very long line of communication, whereas a Hawkeye controlling the battle space was a very short line of communication. Also, the interpretation of all sensors was a capability that was still better processed by humans, as was the flexibility in processing changes in the situational awareness. A UAS processing the same quality of information as a human was not going to happen any time soon. A person in an aircraft was much harder to work against if an electro-magnetic spectrum was denied, and they were more flexible and adaptable. Computers are very good at single tasks and working on complex single tasks. A person could play a computer playing "GO" and the computer would win every time, but it was not possible to for that computer to simultaneously play, and win, both "GO" and chess. When the game changed, the human being adapted where a computer could not.

From the early days, the battlefield general was back behind the front lines, but there was always a person upon the hill collecting information. That information was communicated to the general, who would use that information to determine strategy and tactics in order to control the battle space. That is exactly the role the Hawkeye is fulfilling today. Except that now, crews have sophisticated systems and radars to acquire that information.

There is a place for UAS, however. The MQ-25 is a perfect example of that. The MQ-25 is a tanker, that performs the long, and sometimes tedious, missions that involve waiting for aircraft to need refueling; often, these were the types of missions that do not require manning. The MQ-25s are roughly the size of a Hornet, and, therefore, take up space on the flight deck. Space is critical. Naval Aviation is working out how it can fit more aircraft on a carrier, so size does matter. The new E-2D huffer — an external engine that creates large volumes of pressurized air used to start large gas turbine jet engines on some types of aircraft — requires more space as well, and it is something that must be tackled. How many MQ-25s are assigned to a CAW is unclear and dependent on requirement. The Pentagon is working very hard on this program.

An E-2C Hawkeye squadron usually deploys four aircraft to a carrier. With the advanced capabilities of the E-2D, additional tasks have been added and resulted in the deployment of one additional aircraft during deployment.

Chapter 13
Training Squadron Developments

The operational squadrons bear responsibility for training up their new aircrews to become section and division flight leads. The weapons school at NAS Fallon mostly trains candidates going through the "Top Gun" course or provided training to carrier air wings doing their workups for their deployments at NAS Fallon. The West Coast bases that fulfill the training tasks are NAS Corpus Christi and NAS Kingsville. Both bases are tasked with continuing the training for naval aviator students.

Training Setup

When the Aviation Preflight Indoctrination is successfully completed and the Student Naval Aviators (SNA) graduate, the SNA are assigned to Training Air Wing 6 (TAW-6) at NAS Pensacola, Training Air Wing 5 (TAW-5) at NAS Whiting Field, or Training Air Wing Four (TAW-4) at NAS Corpus Christi. Here, they learn to master the Beechcraft T-6B Texan II. TAW-4 and TAW-5 primarily instruct the basics of flying in approximately six months. Lessons include ground school, in which aircraft systems, local course rules, and emergency procedures are taught.

The contact phase, in which take-off and landing, limited maneuvers, spins, Emergency Landing Pattern (ELP) and emergency procedures are thoroughly trained, in combination with the basic instruments course, includes common instrument scans and generic instrument flight procedures.

Later in the six-month training, the principles of precision aerobatics, such as aileron rolls, loops, Cuban Eights, barrel rolls, wingovers, split S, Immelmann and Cloverleaf maneuvers are taught. This stage also involves training in formation flying, including the basic section flight and cruise formation flight.

The final stage involves radio instrument navigation (VOR, Holding, ILS/LOC, PAR/ASR, and RNAV) and includes night familiarization and visual navigation training flights.

Student Naval Aviators who are destined for carrier-borne types are required to fly a series of Field Carrier Landing Practices (FCLP) at the end of nearly every training mission. This involves them using a marked-out carrier deck on the airfield's runway and flying a circuit pattern and descent rate and speed that is consistent with how it would be flown for real at the carrier deck. This has been designed as part of the building-block process toward their initial carrier qualifications in the T-45C Goshawk.

Student Naval Aviators selected for strike training continue their training at NAS Meridian or NAS Kingsville, operating the T-45C. The intermediate syllabus incorporated basic instrument flying, formation, night familiarization, and airway navigation over approximately 58 graded flights, lasting approximately 27 weeks.

Advanced strike students continue with approximately 67 additional graded flights, lasting approximately 23 weeks in the T-45 Goshawk. The syllabus covered bombing, air combat maneuvering (ACM), advanced instruments, low-level navigation, tactical formation flying (TACFORM), and carrier qualification (CQ).

For the freshly winged aviators graduated from the advanced strike course, their next assignment before arriving at an operational squadron was to go to an FRS. The F/A-18 FRSs were VFA-106 "Gladiators," on the East Coast, and VFA-122 "Flying Eagles," on the West Coast. Pilots selected for the F-35C continued their FRS training with VFA-125 "Rough Raiders" on the West Coast. There, they went through a complete syllabus to learn the basics of operating and tactically employing the aircraft, before they were assigned to an operational squadron. New aviators at the FRS went through a series of familiarization simulators before their first flight in the F/A-18. The first few flights were in a trainer aircraft, but the first solo flight took place much earlier than in the T-34 Mentor, T-6 Texan II, or T-45 Goshawk syllabus. After that point, the "Cones," as the trainees were affectionately referred, progressed through the syllabus, and performed various air-to-surface and air-to-air flights, some of which were conducted as solo and some with an instructor in the back seat. The FRS students were referred to as "Cones" because new F-18 pilots were considered "Category One" (Cat One – C. One – "Cone") students. There were four categories. Cat 1 referred to brand new students flying the F/A-18. The next category, Cat 2, was for pilots with tactical jet experience but transitioning into the F/A-18. Cat 3 and Cat 4 were for F/A-18 pilots that had been out of the cockpit for a certain amount of time.

Modernizing Advanced Flight Training

In the past decade, the primary flight training inventory had been significantly modernized with the replacement of the 1975-introduced Beechcraft T-34C Turbo Mentor by the modern Beechcraft T-6B Texan II. The Texan II was based on the Swiss-designed Pilatus PC-9 trainer.

The advanced flight training operated the McDonnell Douglas T-45 Goshawk, which was the modified version of the British BAE Systems Hawk. The original design of the British Aerospace Hawk jet trainer was specified on a land-based design. The T-45 Goshawk, although severely redesigned, never evolved to possess the requisite handling characteristics to make carrier approaches easier for the pilot. The naval aviators described the T-45C Goshawk as being underpowered and twitchy during the final approach to the aircraft carrier deck.

The T-45C had been in service since 1991 and the Navy, in its quest for continuous improvement of its operations, started the definition stage specifying the requirements for a future advanced flight training program. Between 2019 and 2020, the definition phase of the replacement project was setup, specifying the environment in which the successor of the T-45C Goshawk could facilitate a totally new approach to the training methods for advanced flight training. During the definition phase of the project, the Navy talked to the aviation industry regarding the potential for a new training aircraft to grow into a multi-role platform as a future adversary and, potentially, as a surrogate training aircraft.

Conventionally, the SNA conducted manual approaches to aircraft carriers when operating the T-45C Goshawk during the last stage of their advanced flight training. This required advanced levels of skill and concentration, with posed a significant risk for mishaps and accidents due to the limited flight control systems. The advanced capabilities in the fifth-generation fighters enabled the pilot to land on

Some of the last surviving T-34C Mentors are assigned to the FRS. VFA-122 "Flying Eagles" still has five operational aircraft. Seen here on the NAS Lemoore flight line are three examples, all in a different camouflage scheme.

In 2019, NAF El Centro named its airfield Vraciu Field, in honor of legendary Navy pilot Commander Alexander Vraciu, a World War Two ace with direct ties to the base. El Centro is the host of temporary deployments of squadrons during the autumn and winter season. The T-45C Goshawk is a regular guest at NAF El Centro. Both FRS and active fighter squadron F/A-18 deployments take place on a regular basis. Seen here is a T-45C crew returning from a training sortie.

an aircraft carrier with the integration of Delta Flight Path (DFP) technology, also referred to as "Magic Carpet" technology, now also engineered in the F/A-18 Super Hornet and EA-18 Growler. This took the pressure off the training requirement during advanced flight training and required changes in the training program and the replacement aircraft.

In May 2020, the Navy initiated a new project referred to as its Undergraduate Jet Training System (UJTS). This project included the demanding specifications of carrier flight operations instruction. A request for information (RFI) was released to the aviation industry on May 14, 2020, with the vision to acquire a non-developmental, land-based jet trainer by 2028.

In this RFI, the definition of the replacement aircraft included the possible limitation, and even elimination, of the ability to land and take off from the carrier. Comparable to the T-45C Goshawk, the new trainer aircraft would be limited to conducting FCLP and was not certain in its definition on the requirement for carrier-based touch-and-go approaches and landings. With the addition of the DFP technology, automation would certainly affect the methods in which the Strike Fighter Squadrons performed their landings on carrier decks. As a result, the training of future naval aviators in the skills of cat-and-trap carrier operations, and recertifying fleet pilots during CQ, had been significantly simplified with the use of technology.

The specification for the replacement jet trainer aircraft included the requirement to fly 400 hours each year. The jets would conduct around 1,200 FCLP landings, using simulated carrier decks ashore, as well as up to 45 touch-and-goes on actual carriers, annually. The latest developments also called for a modification in the specification if the Navy decided to also remove the CQ from the requirements. The new, fast jet training aircraft may even no longer be required to fly an FCLP nearly every time it returned to the air station, and it would never need to go to the carrier. As long as new pilots learned the basics, spent plenty of time in the simulator, and flew a sensible number of high sink-rate FCLP approaches, they would graduate; they would then go to their respective FRSs to learn how to fly their operational aircraft type and be introduced to carrier deck landing skills.

Both the F-35 and F/A-18 Hornet squadrons already performed CQ using Precision Landing Mode (PLM), meaning the current "pressure" on performing high-risk carrier deck landings during advanced flight training in an aircraft that is not equipped with the latest state-of-the-art technology was reduced. Eliminating the carrier CQ element, including touch-and-go approaches and landings, would also eliminate the need to heavily modify the UJTS aircraft design, since the requirement to be carrier-capable would be abandoned, allowing for the procurement of a less complex design.

Relying on these systems posed a level of risk as well, however. If the systems were damaged as a result of combat, the naval aviators might be insufficiently experienced to perform manual carrier deck landings.

Compliance to the Navy Vision

The advanced capabilities that PLM offered fulfilled one of the major objectives within the Navy's vision for changes in the way it trained new pilots. The Navy was evaluating whether to exclude carrier qualifications from the advanced flight training syllabus, and would, therefore, not require any carrier flying from its follow-on UJTS training aircraft. This "business efficiency" step significantly reduced required resources in design costs, training program duration, and budgeting, mostly driven by the desired reduction of training timelines and increased naval aviator training efficiency. Instead, Strike Fighter pilots could be trained in carrier flying once at their respective FRSs in an aircraft equipped with the PLM capabilities.

Training new carrier pilots may also involve significant use of simulators. The flight control software in the new trainer could even include a system that was similar to PLM, presenting a much more intuitive transition for pilots between the training squadron and the FRS. This development would not only reduce training timelines, but it would also massively reduce the burden on the already over-tasked aircraft carriers, since the Navy was no longer in the luxurious position of having dedicated training carriers. It also reduced the requirement to support Chief of Naval Air Training (CNTRA) activities.

Recent developments even enabled a slightly reduced demand for complex cat-and-trap training, due to the changing composition of the carrier air wing. The C-2 Greyhound Carrier Onboard Delivery (COD) aircraft was replaced by the CMV-22 Osprey — meaning one less type to include in this style of training. The Osprey landed on a carrier like a helicopter, versus the Greyhound, which relied on the arresting gear to land and the catapult to launch.

A remaining challenge to be further defined was training of the new E-2 Hawkeye pilots. These aircraft were required to perform manual approaches to the carrier, with no technology resembling PLM. Currently, future E-2 Hawkeye pilots have been initially trained on the T-45C Goshawk and, while this currently provides carrier operations familiarity, there is little actual handling crossover in flying a T-45 and flying an E-2. New Hawkeye pilots have the luxury of a safety pilot/instructor sitting alongside them when they learn the ropes, and it is expected that this portion of training would be increased if the Goshawk course no longer included CQ.

Instead, the Navy is defining how the new training aircraft could evolve into a multi-role tasked platform. Operating the modern fourth- and fifth-generation strike fighter aircraft is an expensive endeavor. A substitute aircraft could provide the Navy with a low-cost companion to its frontline fleet fighters, reducing the burden of maintaining the strike fighter fleet to combat-readiness standard. It would also be a huge step in reducing the cost and managing sustainability of future Naval Aviation.

Below left: After a production hiatus of almost 15 years, the T-34C Turbo-Mentor powered by a Pratt & Whitney Canada PT6A-25 turboprop engine was developed in 1973. Development proceeded at the behest of the USN, which supplied two T-34Bs for conversion. After re-engining with the PT6, the two aircraft were redesignated as YT-34Cs, the first of these flying with turboprop power for the first time on September 21, 1973. Mentor production restarted in 1975 for deliveries of T-34Cs to the USN and of the T-34C-1 armed version for export customers in 1977. This version features four underwing hard points. The last Turbo-Mentor rolled off the production line in 1990. The last Mentors are now serving in a supporting role.

Below right: Training Squadron 28 (VT-28) is one of two primary training squadrons located at NAS Corpus Christi. Primary training consists of several instructional phases of flight in the T-6B Texan II single-engine, turboprop, ejection-seat aircraft. The squadron used to be equipped with the T-34C Mentor from 1990–2013. Captured here is BuNo 160647 modex G-730 during a fuel stop at Tucson International Airport in 2013.

The Navy is also further assessing its adversary capability as a potential area where the new replacement trainer aircraft could be integrated. The current adversary aircraft in use are the F-5N/F Tiger II, F-16A/B Fighting Falcon, and the F/A-18 C Legacy Hornet. In the past five years, the Navy started using civil contractors to provide adversary capacity, due to the shortages in internal capacity.

Although the Navy acquired additional ex-Swiss Air Force F-5 Tiger II aircraft, and the first adversary squadrons will make their conversions to the Super Hornet, there is still a significant over demand for adversary capacity. The new jet trainer aircraft could fulfil a modest role in decreasing the gap.

Project Avenger

The development of a new revised training system was managed in a separate project. Named after the World War Two Grumman Avenger torpedo bomber, Project Avenger comprised a new modernized training philosophy using new technology and methods to significantly reduce the training duration. The main purpose was a reduction of the training time to 18 months. Even though the training period would be shortened, it was not the intention to reduce actual flying hours, and it would ultimately generate a better naval aviator due to increased efficiency. The use of Virtual Reality Part-Task Trainer systems was being rolled out first in the T-6B Texan II, and the Navy wanted to repeat this in the follow-on advanced flight training syllabus. However, it acknowledged the move from the T-6 to the T-45 was something of a retrograde step, in terms of advanced learning. The Navy's new training aircraft would be aimed at addressing that requirement for advanced learning, with embedded synthetic training being a vital component.

VMFAT-101 also still operates three T-34C Mentors. Although these aircraft have been assigned to the Marines, the titles on them strongly suggest that the aircraft are assigned to the Navy. It is captured here at NAF El Centro during a fuel stop in October 2019.

Training Air Wing 2 (TAW-2) is responsible for providing the fleet with newly winged Navy and Marine Corps aviators. The air wing consists of approximately 250 Student Naval Aviators, 75 instructor pilots, 80 civilian personnel, and 100 T-45A and T-45C Goshawk aircraft. TAW-2 was introduced at NAS Kingsville in 1992.

Above: In the early spring, TAW-2 regularly deploys to NAF El Centro to provide training in favorable weather conditions. Seen here at NAF El Centro on finals is BuNo 163638 modex B-238.

Left: Training Squadron 27 (VT-27) is assigned to Training Air Wing 4 based at NAS Corpus Christi. The squadron frequently deploys to Laughlin/Bullhead International Airport in Arizona during springtime. Seen in this image is the entire detachment on training in March 2015.

Below left: VT-35 currently operates the T-44C "Pegasus" and is one of two advanced multi-engine training squadrons responsible for providing naval aviators to the US Navy and Marine Corps. After completion of their prescribed syllabus, SNA are assigned to fly the US Navy P-8 Poseidon, EP-3 Aries or the US Marine Corps MV-22 Osprey, previously the TC-12B. This aircraft painted in centennial markings was transferred to 309th AMARG in February 2018.

Below right: BuNo 166790 modex NJ-111 has been assigned to VFA-122 since March 2014.

Above: NAS Lemoore recreated a carrier deck on its runway. Aircrews are able to perform landings like they would on an aircraft carrier, including a Light Signal Officer-directed landing.

Right: From March 1984, when the last T-28B ever used for naval flight training departed, to June 2013, the T-34C was the mainstay of the Navy and Marine Corps primary flight training program. In June 2013, VT-27 "Boomers" transitioned from T-34C to the T-6B Texan II.

Training Squadron 27 was initially established on July 11, 1951, as Advanced Training Unit-B at Naval Air Station Corpus Christi where it remains currently as part of Training Wing 2.

Training Air Wing 4 is one of five training air wings under the Chief of Naval Air Training Command and was established in March 1972. Four individual squadrons make up the wing. They are VT-27, VT-28, VT-31, and VT-35.

Above: TW-2 is a United States Navy aircraft training air wing based at NAS Kingsville. TW-2 is one of five training air wings in the Naval Air Training Command and consists of two jet training squadrons, Training Squadron 21 (VT-21) and Training Squadron 22 (VT-22). The wing trains SNA from the US Navy, US Marine Corps, and international allies. Following completion of primary flight training and selection of an advanced training pipeline, Student Naval Aviators are assigned to TW-2 for either intermediate and advanced strike pipeline training or advanced E-2/C-2 training in the T-45C Goshawk jet training aircraft.

Below left: Introduced to NAS Kingsville in 1992, the Goshawk is part of the T-45 Training System (TS) developed by McDonnell Douglas, now Boeing Aircraft Company.

Below right: VT-22 "Golden Eagles," using radio callsign "Blazer," is equipped with the T-45C Goshawk and the squadron operates from Naval Air Station Kingsville. The squadron received its first T-45A Goshawks in 1994 and still operates this type, although it has been upgraded to the T-45C standard.

Chapter 14
Naval Air Warfare Development Center Developments

Advanced tactical training for all naval aviators is currently provided at the NAWDC at NAS Fallon.

The Birth of Top Gun

In 1968, Chief of Naval Operations (CNO) Admiral Thomas Hinman Moorer ordered Captain Frank Ault to research the poor statistics of the Navy and Marine fighter crews in Vietnam, which were losing one fighter for every two adversary MiG aircraft they shot down. The investigation would mainly focus on the disappointing performance of the air-to-air missiles used in combat in the skies over North Vietnam. The USAF earlier concluded that its air losses were primarily due to unobserved MiG attacks from the rear, and were, therefore, a technology problem. The service responded by upgrading its F-4 Phantom II fleet, installing an internal M61 Vulcan cannon, replacing of the gun pods carried under the aircraft's belly by Air Force Phantom squadrons, developing improved airborne radar systems, and working to solve the targeting problems of the AIM-9 and AIM-7 air-to-air missiles.

In May 1968, the Navy published the *Ault Report* which concluded that the problem stemmed from inadequate aircrew training in air combat maneuvering. This was welcomed by the F-8 Crusader community. The F-8 Crusader, though aging, had a gun integrated into its design that the Navy F-4 Phantom aircraft were lacking. Among its wide-ranging recommendations to improve air combat performance, the *Ault Report* recommended that an "Advanced Fighter Weapons School" had to be established at Naval Air Station Miramar to revive and disseminate community fighter expertise throughout the fleet.

The main reason for the disappointing results was that the Navy F-4 Phantoms were not equipped with a gun, and aircrews were heavily depending on their missiles. The missiles, however, were not very reliable and only a low percentage of the missiles struck their target. Due to the lack of training of the aircrews in advanced air combat, the Navy suffered heavy losses.

The Naval Fighter Weapons School, Top Gun, was formed on March 3, 1969, using the F-4 Phantoms of FRS VF-121 "Pacemakers." Eight instructors and one intelligence officer were hand-picked by the school's first officer-in-charge, Lieutenant Commander Dan A Pedersen. This initial staff designed the Naval Fighter Weapons School syllabus, improving the quality of the syllabus as time progressed. Their primary mission was to train fighter aircrews at the graduate level in all aspects of fighter weapons systems including tactics, techniques, procedures, and doctrine.

Dissimilar Air Combat Training (DACT) was introduced and focused almost exclusively on the air-to-air mission by Dan Pedersen's group. Its objective was to develop, refine, and teach aerial dogfight tactics and techniques to certain fleet aircrews, using the DACT concept.

The first courses took four weeks, in which multiple training missions were conducted to gain the required experience. The F-4 Phantom II crews flew their missions against the agile A-4 Skyhawk and

The F-16s assigned to NAWDC were originally destined to be delivered to Pakistan. When the Foreign Military Sales program was canceled, the aircraft were initially transferred to storage at 309th AMARG at Davis-Monthan Air Force Base. The aircraft, however, were soon assigned to NAWDC, initially in their original two-tone grey camouflage scheme. This was soon to be replaced by a two-tone blue and two-tone brown scheme.

The Naval Air Warfare Development Center (NAWDC) has a large variety of aircraft within its operational inventory. The squadron fulfills a major role in the air-to-air combat training of the active fighter squadrons, providing real-time scenarios for the crews attending Top Gun classes and carrier air wing training. Training often takes place in close cooperation with VFC-13, who fulfill the adversary role.

T-38 Talon aircraft. The aircrews that attended the initial Top Gun courses were crews from frontline squadrons, who would transfer their knowledge and experience to the other crews within their squadrons. When the first classes graduated, the crews deployed back to their operational squadrons. During the pauses in the North Vietnam campaign, Top Gun established itself as a center of excellence in fighter doctrine, tactics, and training. By the time aerial activity over North Vietnam resumed, most Navy squadrons had a Top Gun graduate. The results became apparent quickly, significantly increasing the Navy kill-to-loss ratio against the North Vietnamese Air Force (NVAF) from 2.42 to 1, to a ratio of 12.5 to 1.

The success developed Top Gun into a separate, fully funded command, with its own permanently assigned aircraft, staffing, and infrastructural assets.

Expanding the Top Gun Legacy

In the 1970s and 1980s, the F-4 Phantom II within the Naval Strike Fighter Squadrons was replaced by the F-14 Tomcat and the F/A-18 Hornet. Both aircraft were fitted with an on-board gun, further emphasizing the need for advanced fighter training. The instructors at Top Gun retained A-4 Skyhawks and F-5E Tiger II aircraft but later added the F-16 Fighting Falcon to better simulate the threat presented by the Soviet Union's new fourth-generation Mikoyan Gurevich MiG-29 Fulcrum and Sukhoi Su-27 Flanker fighters. However, the specially built F-16N developed cracks in the airframe and were retired early.

Largely due to the end of the Cold War in the early 1990s, the Top Gun syllabus was modified to include more emphasis on the air-to-ground strike mission, due to the expanding multi-mission taskings of the F-14 and F/A-18. In addition, Top Gun retired its A-4 Skyhawks and F-5E Tiger IIs in favor of F-16 Fighting Falcons assigned to VF-45 "Blackbirds" and F/A-18 Hornets assigned to VFA-127 "Royal Blues," assigned to the adversary or "Aggressor" squadrons. VF-45 was deactivated on March 31, 1996, and VFA-127 was deactivated March 23, 1996, as a result of the planned relocation to NAS Fallon.

Move from the Sea to the Desert

In 1996, Top Gun was integrated into the NAWDC and was relocated to NAS Fallon. NAS Miramar changed to a Marine Corps air station and all Navy squadrons moved out. NAS Fallon was selected, given the closeness of the required practice ranges nearby, enabling the crews to practice the multi-role missions in one designated area. The Fallon Range Training Complex includes more than 10,200 square miles of airspace and ground bombing areas, all covered by an array of computer-aided electronic systems that record each mission for post-flight analysis.

The need to improve air-to-ground, as well as air-to-air skills, was why the program was relocated to NAS Fallon, where the operational squadrons could practice strike missions and really reset focus to the basics. The Naval Air Warfare Center evolved Top Gun, which initially focused on air-to-air combat, into "Strike U" by adding the ground attack missions.

In 2002, the Navy received 14 F-16A and B aircraft from the Aerospace Maintenance and Regeneration Center (AMARC) that were originally intended for the Pakistan Air Force before being embargoed. These aircraft were assigned to NAWDC for adversary training.

Top Gun Classes

Top Gun conducted four "Power Projection" classes a year. Each class lasted nine weeks and consisted of nine Navy and Marine Corps strike fighter aircraft. The Top Gun course was designed to train experienced Navy and Marine Corps aircrews at the graduate level to all aspects of strike-fighter aircraft employment. This includes tactics, hardware, techniques, and the current world threat for air-to-air and air-to-ground missions. The course included 80 hours of lectures and 25 sorties, in which the students trained against Top Gun instructors. When the aircrew completed the course, the crewmembers would return as training officers, carrying the latest tactical doctrine back to their operational squadron or going directly to a Fleet Replacement Squadron to teach new aircrews. Strike Fighter Tactics Instructors (SFTI) could also become instructors themselves at Top Gun at a later stage in their career.

Top Gun also trained four to six Air Intercept Controllers (AIC) in each class on advanced command, control, and combat communication skills. They were completely integrated into the course and participated in most of the training missions. These AIC students, some of whom were E-2C/D Hawkeye naval flight officers, returned to their carrier air wings after graduation and were given the responsibility of training all the air controllers and fighters in their carrier strike groups in the art of air intercept control.

The F-16 aircraft assigned to NAWDC can project a Dissimilar Air Combat Training scenario, similar to the F-5E Tiger II in use by VFC-13, with the difference being that the F-16 is a fourth-generation aircraft capable to project a more enhanced scenario to the Navy aircrews.

Top Gun also conducted an Adversary Training Course, flying with an adversary aircrew from each Navy and Marine Corps adversary squadron. These pilots received individual instruction in threat simulation, effective threat presentation, and adversary tactics. Top Gun provided academics and flight training to each carrier air wing during its Integrated and Advanced Training Phases (ITP/ATP) at NAS Fallon, which were large-scale exercises that could involve as many as 50 aircraft. These large-scale exercises served as "pre-deployment rehearsals" for future combat scenarios. In addition to training crews, Top Gun also conducted ground school courses six times a year. The Training Officer Ground School (TOGS) offered graduate-level academics to fleet aviators, adversary instructors, and other officers and enlisted personnel.

Top Gun also provided a Strike-Fighter Tactics Refresher Course, also referred to as "Re-Blue," once a year, usually in the fall, bringing current fleet SFTIs back to Fallon for a two-day refresher and updating of the Top Gun recommendations.

The Top Gun course changed significantly over the last 50 years, adapting and continuously improving the syllabus to the latest techniques in modern air combat. In the 1970s, the course lasted four weeks, extended to five weeks in the 1980s. The final F-4 Phantoms completed their class in March 1985, and the final F-14 Tomcats in October 2003. Programs formerly run by Top Gun that were transferred to other commands, or discontinued, include Fleet Air Superiority Training (FAST) and Hornet Fleet Air Superiority Training (HFAST).

Evolving to NAWDC

Prior to June 2015, NAWDC was known as Naval Strike and Air Warfare Center (NSAWC), which was the consolidation of three commands into a single command structure on July 11, 1996. NSAWC was a composition of the Naval Strike Warfare Center, referred to as STRIKE "U," based at NAS Fallon since 1984, and two schools from NAS Miramar, the Top Gun Navy Fighter Weapons School and the Top Dome Carrier Airborne Early Warning Weapons School. The name was changed to align with the naming convention of the Navy's other Warfare Development Centers, including the Naval Surface and Mine Warfare Development Center (SMWDC) and the Undersea Warfare Development Center (UWDC).

Currently, NAWDC operates a wide variety of aircraft, enabling NAWDC to train the aircrews in each individual aspect of air warfare. In the current setup, NAWDC weapons schools also sharpen the combat skills of crews for E-2C carrier airborne early warning planes, H-60 helicopters, EA-18G electronic warfare jets and, recently, also added the fifth-generation F-35C to its operational inventory. The center also produces planners and managers who can devise and execute complex air campaigns.

NAWDC is dedicated to continuously improving Naval Aviation, from the individual pilot and crewmember up to the integrated warfighting instrument of the carrier air wing and the associated air, sea, and land components.

F-16A BuNo 920408 is seen here in a two-tone brown camouflage scheme, landing after a successful carrier air wing training scenario in October 2018. The aircraft has a non-standard BuNo since it is derived from the Foreign Military Sales serial number originally assigned to the aircraft, 90-0408.

Refocusing, Back to the Future

After a decade of Naval Aviation conducting primarily counterinsurgency ground support missions with no anti-air threat, the NAWDC training program was modified. NAWDC integrated enhanced, high-end warfighting skills throughout a greater percentage of the duration of the courses. Naval Air Forces adapted very well to the missions they were conducting, but as a result from the integral effort, some of the higher-end skills, like air-to-air missions and higher-end opposed strike missions, had not been trained with the same high level of effort. NAWDC was starting to refocus on these core values, because of the enhanced capabilities of potential future adversaries, in both the East and Far East.

While Top Gun was recognized for its work in teaching high-end air-to-air combat skills, its fellow Airborne Electronic Attack Weapons School, also referred to as "Havoc", tended to move in the shadows. This elite school prepared EA-18G Growler aircrews for modern-day air combat, following the same doctrine as Top Gun. While the traditional techniques of air-to-air and air-to-ground employment of fighter aircraft were well documented, the EA-18G Growlers electronic attack mission remained compared with an electronic wizard. The Growler brought the most advanced tactical electronic warfare capabilities to operational commanders, creating a tactical advantage for friendly air, land, and maritime forces by delaying, degrading, denying, or deceiving enemy electronic warfare systems.

Like Top Gun, Havoc was part of NAWDC, and it was tucked away in the same nondescript building at one end of the long flight line at NAS Fallon in Nevada. Despite the lack of fanfare, just like its sister organization, Havoc's activities were at the forefront of modern Naval Aviation.

Airborne Electronic Attack (AEA) essentially involved the offensive and defensive suppression of an enemy's electromagnetic spectrum, including radars and communications. AEA included the ability to monitor hostile electromagnetic activity, as well as to evaluate, disrupt, manipulate, and even disable the related systems. These could be the nodes that typically formed part of an Integrated Air Defense System (IADS), which could collect tracking data and disseminate it to various "shooters," such as surface-to-air missile sites, that were then able to tackle an incoming threat. The ability to confuse, and even suppress or disable IADS, meant that its engagement ability was seriously degraded, or some parts of it could even be wiped out entirely.

The primary role of Havoc was providing training to the Growler Tactics Instructors (GTI) that form the main drive of the EA-18G community. The training aimed to efficiently optimize the use of the Growlers sensors and weapons. In addition, it trained intelligence officers, who similarly received the highest level of EA-18G tactical qualification. The intelligence shops were responsible for providing the latest data on threat systems, so the aircrews, and their enhanced electronic warfare systems, knew exactly how to deal with and counter them.

NAWDC is the center of excellence for US Navy training and tactics development, with Havoc being a department within this large organization, and known officially as N10. Havoc tracked the EA-18G's

Two very colorful NAWDC F16s are taxiing to the NAS Fallon runway, In order to take part in the large force exercise scenario during a carrier air wing training in October 2018.

path and growth within US Navy service and will mark its tenth anniversary in 2021 – a decade that was geared toward maintaining the Growler's leading edge in the complexities of the AEA mission.

The Havoc course had three main phases. The course included air-to-air training with a strong focus on electronic attack, an air-to-ground phase also focused on electronic attack, and an additional capstone exercise phase that was provided at Nellis AFB. The crews deployed to Nellis AFB for a month, operating alongside the Air Force Weapons School in its Weapons School Integration (WSINT) phase, also referred to as "wizz-int." During this phase, the Havoc students worked closely with the Air Force Suppression of Enemy Air Defense (SEAD) F-16 Fighting Falcons and the fifth-generation F-22 Raptors and F-35 Lightning.

In addition to the GTI course at NAS Fallon, the Navy had a Growler Electronic Attack Weapons School (EAWS) at NAS Whidbey Island. This school was first established in 1974, within Attack Squadron VA-128 "Golden Intruders," to provide refresher and advanced courses for Grumman A-6 Intruder ordnance personnel. This evolved into a course for weapons and advanced strike planning.

The GTI course consisted of academic, simulator, and live flight events on both the Fallon Range Training Complex and the Nevada Test and Training Range. Graduates of the GTI course became instructors at Havoc or EAWS. After those two-year instructor tours, they returned to fleet squadrons as Training Officers, where they became the connective tissue between the tactics developed at Havoc and fleet aircrew employing the full range of Growler capabilities.

The integration of the F-35 Lighting within the Navy will play an increasingly vital role, in which data exchange, in combination with the enhanced capabilities of stealth technology, will also have a huge influence on NAWDC and the continuous improvement in the development of air warfare doctrine and the tailor-made training methods.

NAWDC also operates two E-2C+ aircraft. These aircraft are used in the large force exercise scenarios, acting as "Red Air." The Hawkeyes are also used for the Hawkeye Weapons and Tactics Instructor (HEWTI) course and for developing tactics and techniques for the E-2 community. They also provide support for other NAWDC development and training programs.

Below left: The Specialized and Proven Aircraft Program office (PMA-226) completed a modification on ten US NAWDC F-16A Fighting Falcon adversary aircraft at NAS Fallon. The modification, named FalconUP, increased the readiness and service life of the Fighting Falcons with more than 500 hours. The FalconUP modification also provided the configuration baseline to incorporate the funded Structural Augmentation Roadmap (Falcon STAR) program, which adds an additional 3,750 hours to the service life of the aircraft. The Falcon STAR was already provided to the US Air Force (and completed in FY2015), but the US Navy Fighting Falcons are still slated for this upcoming modification program.

Below right: Prior to their taxi run at NAS Fallon, all required aircraft for that day's sortie are lined up.

Naval Air Warfare Development Center Developments

Above left: The Legacy Hornets have all been withdrawn from use in operational Naval fighter squadrons. A few Legacy Hornets remain in service with NAWDC. Some of these aircraft have been painted in an adversary color scheme. BuNo 164013 modex 20 is painted in a two-tone brown scheme.

Above right: Gradually, the aging Legacy Hornets are finding their way into AMARG. BuNo 164066 modex 20 is painted in a two-tone blue scheme and arrived at 309th AMARG on May 6, 2019.

Right: The NAWDC ramp is home to a range of different aircraft types, which represent the diversity (or more accurately, the lack thereof) of types within Naval Aviation today. Clearly, versions of the F/A-18 Hornet make up the bulk of the US Navy's tactical fleet, and NAWDC has examples of both Legacy and Super Hornets, along with a small fleet of EA-18G Growlers.

Below: This F/A-18E assigned to NAWDC clearly presents the Naval Fighter Weapons School, also known as Top Gun, emblem on the tail.

Chapter 15

Helicopter Sea Combat and Maritime Strike Squadron Developments

Over the past decade, the Navy continued to reduce the high variety in aircraft and helicopter types within its inventory. In 2010, the Navy was developing a helicopter concept of operations which involved the deployment of full squadrons of the multi-mission MH-60S and MH-60R, to be integrated in the Carrier Strike Groups, as well as detachments on board cruisers, destroyers, and frigates.

MH-XX was the recapitalization effort of the maritime capabilities currently provided by the MH-60S and MH-60R. From 2010 until 2014, a major push was given to the MH-XX program. Lockheed Martin was awarded a contract in September 2010 to develop software for MH-60R and MH-60S helicopters, followed by another contract in January 2011 for supplying advance spectrum systems for deployment in the MH-60R by April 2013. Also in January 2011, Lockheed Martin was awarded a contract comprising the production and development for an MH-60R fleet. Lockheed Martin also secured a five-year contract to deliver more than 200 digital cockpits and integrated mission systems and sensors for the US Navy MH-60R and MH-60S helicopters in April 2012.

With the MH-XX initiative, the Navy standardized its Sea Combat and Maritime Strike capabilities to the MH-60S and MH-60R helicopters. Redesigned from an SH-60B, the first MH-60R helicopter made its first flight in July 2001. The first two new-build MH-60R helicopters were delivered to the US Navy in August 2005. The first Helicopter Maritime Strike Squadron, HSM-71, equipped with MH-60R, was established by the US Navy at NAS North Island in October 2007. By November 2014, the Navy received its 200th MH-60R.

The MH-60S was originally designated CH-60S, as a replacement for the Navy dual-rotored Boeing CH-46D Sea Knight heavy-lift helicopters in the vertical replenishment role. The helicopter was redesignated MH-60S, as a result of an expansion in mission requirements to include a range of additional combat support capabilities. Retirement of the Sea Knights concluded in September 2004. Sikorsky was awarded the US Navy contract to develop the MH-60S in 1997. The production aircraft made its maiden flight in January 2000. The operational evaluation began in November 2001 at the Naval Air Warfare Centre at Patuxent River, Maryland, and concluded in May 2002.

Besides the five MH-60S helicopters that NAWDC operates, NAS Fallon also has three MH-60S assigned to the search and rescue squadron. Seen in this image is BuNo 166296 modex 7H-04.

The MH-60S conducted surface and mine countermeasures, as well as combat search and rescue, logistics, and Special Operations Forces support. For this, they were equipped with the following: Link-16 data link, advanced forward-looking infrared system, airborne laser mine detecting and mine neutralization systems, precision air-to ground missiles, 20mm fixed forward-firing gun, and crew served machine guns. The MH-60S deployed with CSGs, ARGs, and littoral combat ships.

The MH-60R conducted surface and subsurface warfare with data links, Hawk Link and Link-16, airborne low-frequency dipping sonar, sonobuoys, inverse synthetic aperture radar with automatic periscope detection and discrimination modes, electronic support measures, advanced forward-looking infrared system, precision air-to-ground missiles, machine guns, and lightweight torpedoes. Critical to ensuring maritime dominance, the MH-60R was the only airborne anti-submarine warfare asset within strike groups and on independently deploying warships.

The MH-60R and MH-60S Seahawk multi-mission combat helicopters were the pillars of the 21st century rotary air wing within the Navy. These two variants shared 85 percent common components to facilitate maintenance and logistics support. Carrier air wing squadrons deployed on aircraft carriers and strike group escort ships under the leadership of carrier air wing commanders. Expeditionary squadrons deployed as detachments embarked on amphibious assault ships (LHAs/LHDs), surface combatants, and logistics vessels.

Unmanned rotary capabilities were also introduced within the operational inventory of the Navy. The MQ-8 Fire Scout System was designed to operate from suitably equipped air-capable ships. Currently employed as an organic ISR asset, it employed an electro-optical and infrared system, automatic identification system, and other modular mission payloads. Two air vehicles, MQ-8B or MQ-8C, filled gaps in surface and mine countermeasures mission sets with a range of up to 115 nautical miles, an endurance of five to eight hours and the synergistic capability to simultaneously operate a tandem of two airframes, a MH-60 and a MQ-8, from a single ship.

The MQ-8 Fire Scout System was maintained by members of a composite MQ-8/MH-60 aviation detachment and fielded from expeditionary helicopter squadrons Helicopter Maritime Strike (HSM) and Helicopter Sea Combat (HSC). HX-21 performed the initial testing with the drone and, by the end of 2020, the MQ-8B was assigned to squadrons HSC-22, HSC-23, HSM-35, HSM-46, HSM-60, and HSM-72.

In November 2014, LCS-3 USS *Fort Worth* deployed with a single MQ-8B and a single MH-60R to provide airborne support for surface warfare missions. This marked the first time a composite detachment operationally deployed from a littoral combat ship (LCS). The MQ-8B continued to support LCSs until the MQ-8C completed its test and evaluation and then joined the MQ-8B in support of the LCS Program of Record. The MQ-8C provided increased airborne endurance and payload carrying capacity over the MQ-8B while providing the same ISR capabilities. The MQ-8C completed its first flight in October 2013 and achieved IOC in late FY2018.

The helicopter squadron HSC-15 used to be assigned to Carrier Air Wing 17. Founded as HS-15 in 1971, the squadron was decommissioned in 2017, transferring its helicopters to the remaining squadrons.

Above left: HSM-41 is the US Navy's West Coast FRS, training the Navy's newest naval aviators and aircrew to fly and fight the MH-60R helicopter, the world's most advanced rotary wing maritime strike platform.

Above right: Another MH-60S Seahawk assigned to the SAR Lemoore "Wranglers" is BuNo 166339 modex 7S-02. The helicopter was still painted in the regular Navy grey colors and only presented orange SAR titles instead of the standard white/orange DayGlo scheme.

Above: HSM-51 "Warlords" is the Navy's premiere forward-deployed Sikorsky MH-60R "Seahawk" helicopter squadron. Homeported in Naval Air Facility Atsugi, Japan, the "Warlords" provide combat-ready armed anti-surface and anti-submarine helicopter detachments to ships deployed in the Korean, Western Pacific, and Persian Gulf regions.

Below: HSM-73 "Battlecats'" primary mission is to conduct sea control operations in open ocean and littoral environments as an integral part of a carrier air wing with a core on board the carrier and MH-60R detachments on board surface combatants.

The MH-60R is the Navy's new primary maritime dominance helicopter, replacing the SH-60B and SH-60F aircraft. Greatly enhanced over its predecessors, the MH-60R helicopter features a glass cockpit and significant mission system improvements, which give it unmatched capability as an airborne multi-mission naval platform.

Right: HSC-15 was deactivated on March 31, 2017, as a result of the decommissioning of Carrier Air Wing 14. Its helicopters were reassigned over the remaining helicopter squadrons. BuNo 168530 has been transferred to HSC-6.

Below: The Navy Rotary Wing Weapons School at NAWDC instructs graduate-level rotary wing employment through the "SEAWOLF" Seahawk Weapons and Tactics Instructor (SWTI) course and operates five MH-60S Seahawks.

Above: The NAWDC Seahawks all have a distinctive camouflage scheme applied. This specific aircraft is referred to as "the Gecko" given its appearance.

Left: HSC-23 "Wildcards" is a United States Navy helicopter squadron based at NAS North Island. The "Wildcards" operates the MH-60S Seahawk helicopter and the MQ-8B Firescout VTUAV.

Below: In an Anti-Submarine Warfare (ASW) role, HSM-49 "Scopions" uses radar, Electronic Support Measures (ESM), sonobuoys, and ship sensors to localize, classify, track, and, if necessary, attack when a submarine has been detected. Aircraft can be equipped with various different torpedoes for the mission.

Chapter 16

Naval Test and Evaluation Developments

Throughout United States Naval Aviation, there were specific squadrons and teams that had common goals in order to strengthen and continuously improve operations. These squadrons ensured that military personnel had the equipment and technology they needed to succeed at every mission put before them. It was for this reason that the Navy Test and Evaluations Squadron operated, using aircraft to complete its missions and help advance the technology and equipment used by Naval Aviation.

For a successful integration of new aircraft, new modernized systems, and new capabilities, a concept development process applied. This process guided the entire effort from design to the commissioning phase before the new technology was successfully integrated into the operational squadrons. The integral nature of the process also involved writing instructions and a syllabus for the future training of the aircrews.

Commander Operational Test and Evaluation Force

The Naval Test and Evaluation capability was subordinate to a separate command and reports to Commander, Operational Test and Evaluation Force (COMOPTEVFOR). This command provided test and evaluation policy interpretation, implementation, and standardization across all warfare and support divisions. This included the training needed by the Navy to learn and comply with current planning, test, evaluation, and reporting standards. The command's requirements for Defense Acquisition University (DAU) courses and certifications were managed by Policy Division.

From its formation until the early 1970s, OPTEVFOR was an operational command reporting to the Commander in Chief of the Atlantic Fleet (CINCLANTFLT). Its mission was primarily concerned with fleet introduction of new weapons systems, including operational test and evaluation and development of tactics. In 1971, however, OPTEVFOR was designated as the sole independent Navy agency for operational test and evaluation. This move was in response to Congressional and Secretary of Defense initiatives, aimed at improving the defense material acquisition process. The command retained its former responsibilities and added the new ones of making early, independent assessments of operational suitability during the Research and Development (R&D) process. In keeping with these new responsibilities, this moved the participation of OPTEVFOR ahead of the production decision, and the Force Commander began reporting directly to the Chief of Naval Operations.

By late 2015, the US Navy had three Vikings remaining operational in support roles, operated by VX-30 at NAS Point Mugu. One was moved to The Boneyard in Tucson, Arizona, in November 2015. The final two were retired – one stored and the other transferred to NASA, on January 11, 2016, officially retiring the S-3 from Navy service.

In order to carry out its mission, OPTEVFOR must closely follow all R&D programs of the Navy material establishment and in Navy laboratories. Accordingly, CNO authorized direct liaison between COMOPTEVFOR and the heads of developing agencies for all technical matters relating to Navy research, development, test, and evaluation. The staff of COMOPTEVFOR was organized along flexible lines, which gave primary consideration to type of warfare and project administration. Evaluation of equipment and systems was carried out by personnel with experience in the type of equipment or warfare over which their divisions had cognizance.

Additionally, COMOPTEVFOR supported three detachments: COMOPTEVFOR Detachment Edwards AFB, as part of the F-35 Joint Operational Test Team; COMOPTEVFOR Detachment Dahlgren in support of AEGIS Combat Systems testing; and COMOPTEVFOR Detachment San Diego, which coordinated fleet scheduling of operational testing with Pacific Fleet units.

COMOPTEVFOR also coordinated test and evaluation activities with the operational test agencies of the other services and with the Director, Operational Test and Evaluation (DOT&E), who established operational test policy for the DoD. Additionally, the Policy Directorate coordinated multi-service operational test policy with the US Army, US Marine Corps, and US Air Force operational test agencies and was the primary liaison with Congressional staffs, Government Accounting Office, and other outside agencies.

Test and Evaluation Capabilities

There are three Navy Test and Evaluation squadrons based on the West Coast. VX-9 "Vampires" and VX-31 "Dust Devils," based on NAWS China Lake and a separate detachment based at Edwards AFB, and VX-30 "Bloodhounds," based on NAS Point Mugu. All three squadrons have a specific area of focus implementing and commissioning new technology within the operational squadrons.

VX-9, originally Air Development Squadron 5 (VX-5), was commissioned on June 18, 1951, at NAS Moffett Field. VX-9 "Vampires," currently based at NAWS China Lake, is tasked with the testing and evaluation of weapons and their related systems in direct support of the United States Naval Aviation Fleet. The main focus of VX-9 is to adapt to the dynamic testing environment that the aviation field provides.

VX-9 "Vampires" is directly subordinated to COMOPTEVOR. The remaining two West Coast Test and Evaluation squadrons are subordinated to Naval Air Warfare Center Weapons Division (NAWCWD). VX-30 "Bloodhounds" and its sister squadron, VX-31 "Dust Devils," make up the two components of the Naval Test Wing Pacific.

VX-30 "Bloodhounds" was formed in May 1995. VX-30 is a weapons test squadron whose mission is to provide research, development, test, and evaluation of manned and unmanned fixed and rotary wing aircraft and weapons systems. To accomplish its mission, VX-30 operates a diverse inventory of manned aircraft, including NC-37A Gulfstream, P-3C Orion, one remaining NP-3D Orion by the end of 2020, and KC-130T Hercules aircraft. Additionally, the "Bloodhounds" are the Navy's premier West Coast test facility for Unmanned Air Systems (UAS), currently operating the RQ-23A TigerShark.

The VX-30 "Bloodhound" aircraft accomplish range surveillance, photometric support, area clearance, and airborne telemetry on the Naval Air Systems Command Sea Test Range. Project officers

NAS China Lake hosts the Operational Air Test and Evaluation Squadron VX-9, nicknamed the "Vampires." VX-9's mission has grown to include the operational evaluation of attack, fighter, and electronic warfare aircraft, weapons systems and equipment, and to develop tactical procedures for their employment.

lead several weapon system developmental test programs for the fleet. The Airborne Threat Simulation Detachment routinely deploys worldwide to meet unique weapon testing needs at remote ranges and to provide fleet support.

The second West Coast squadron assigned to NAWCWD is VX-31 "Dust Devils." Its main mission is conducting safe, effective, and efficient test flights, providing aircraft, test pilots, project officers, and flight test planning oversight for research, development, test, and evaluation of current and future manned aircraft, weapons, and weapons systems. The goal of the "Dust Devils" is to act as an air test and evaluation squadron. VX-31 operates under the same principles as VX-30 "Bloodhounds," but it has slightly different goals and missions. The VX-31 squadron is not a weapons test squadron but does conduct research and testing, just as the VX-30 squadron does.

All three squadrons will remain playing a vital role in the successful implementation of new and modified aircraft and systems into the operational fleet ensuring the operational squadrons have fully tested and commissioned new systems with a strong focus on continuous improvement.

VX-30 also operates the fleet's only "Billboard" NP-3D – a P-3A upgraded with a large billboard-esqe radar, which can provide over-the-horizon radar capabilities. The NP-3D aircraft were also used to support five NASA Space Shuttle missions, using the Cast Glance optical system to monitor reentry.

Right: VX-30 still operates some P-3C AIPs out of NAS Point Mugu, while the single NP-3D returned to the squadron from depot level maintenance in Waco, Texas, on April 23, 2020.

Below: Test and evaluation squadron VX-30 "Bloodhounds" used to operate a modest variety of P-3C Orions. With most of the P-3C Orions now transferred to the AMARG, this P-3C AIP was still operational in June 2017 taxiing to the NAS Point Mugu runway for another test flight.

Chapter 17
Adversary Developments

The Navy operates a total of five adversary squadrons, mainly consisting of F-5N, F-16, and F/A-18 aircraft. The Navy has three actual adversary squadrons, a reserve strike fighter squadron operating as an adversary squadron, and the aircraft assigned to NAWDC at its disposal. These squadrons provide adversary training for both the Fleet Replacement Squadrons and the Strike Fighter Advanced Readiness Programs.

The Strike Fighter Advanced Readiness Programs (SFARP) are mainly conducted at NAS Fallon. They are also referred to as "workups" for a future deployment on an aircraft carrier. Two different training programs can be identified. There is a basic workup program and a larger force exercise workup, preparing the carrier air wing for an actual cruise.

Several sources speculated on an expansion of adversary capabilities and/or modernization of the aircraft currently in the inventory of the adversary squadrons. These speculations came forth from the higher-level discussion on what to do with US Navy adversary squadrons. The existing squadrons were well established and currently there were no plans to form additional squadrons or to deactivate any of the existing squadrons. Speculations were that this might change within five or ten years, especially with the increasing role of external civilian contractors.

The United States Navy carrier air wings are continuously improving their operational readiness skills and tactics. By submitting the aircrews of the carrier air wings to adversary training during a workup cycle, the crews can further develop their skills in real-time scenarios. This adversary training takes place during a four-week period in which twice-a-day missions are conducted.

Adversary Navy Squadrons

The USN operates a total of three reserve adversary squadrons (VFC-111, VFC-12, VFC-13), while the USMC operates one reserve adversary squadron (VMFA-401). These squadrons consist of F-5N and F/A-18 aircraft. The Navy has an additional reserve strike fighter squadron (VFA-204) that also operates as an adversary squadron, utilizing its F/A-18s. The F/A-18s and F-16s assigned to the NAWDC are also used primarily as aggressors, providing additional adversary assets to USN aviators.

VFC-111, based at NAS Key West, primarily provides adversary support in simulated fighter combat, as well as multiple aircraft strike exercises. This squadron mainly provides adversary support to the relatively new pilots that are trained on the F/A-18 Hornet in the two FRSs. These are VFA-106 "Gladiators" on the East Coast and VFA-122 "Flying Eagles" on the West Coast. VFC-111 "Sundowners" squadron is equipped with the F-5N and provides dissimilar air combat training.

VFC-13 "Saints" provides the "Red Air" adversary role during the Top Gun classes and the carrier air wing work up training programs. These aircraft were featured in the film *Top Gun*, as the latest state-of-the-art MiG-28s. This F-5F served a full operational career as an F-5E, serial number J-3055, with the Swiss Air Force before it was purchased by the US Navy and converted to an F-5F.

The United States Navy Reserve Strike Fighter Squadron, VFA-204 "River Rattlers," based at Naval Air Station Joint Reserve Base New Orleans, is a Naval Air Reserve Force (COMNAVAIRESFOR) squadron and is equipped with the F/A-18A+ Hornet. It provides and supplements the same service by sending both personnel and aircraft to both NAS Key West and NAS Fallon.

Another East Coast-based adversary squadron is VFC-12 "Fighting Omars," subordinated to COMNAVAIRESFOR, also operating the F/A-18A+ Hornet. It will make the transition to F/A-18E/F throughout 2021. The primary task of this squadron is to provide adversary training to the Strike Fighter Advanced Readiness Program (SFARP), responsible for training operational fleet F/A-18 Hornet squadrons. Equal to VFA-204, the "Fighting Omars" supports the F/A-18 FRS at NAS Oceana and is often detached to NAS Key West.

VFC-13 "Fighting Saints" is based at NAS Fallon and is the current program manager of the F5N within the Navy. The squadron's present-day mission includes support locations from coast to coast, in fulfillment of professional fleet adversary support. The "Saints" primarily provide adversary support for FRS, carrier air wings, SFARP, and Navy Special Warfare training. With the formation of VFC-111, the tasks of training the FRSs were transferred to them. The squadron cooperates with assets from NAWDC, VFA-204, and VFC-12 in order to perform its specified tasks. The squadron also provides dissimilar air combat training for the Top Gun classes that are organized at NAS Fallon.

VFC-13 used to have a regular detachment at NAS Key West until the Navy decided to reform the former VF-111 "Sundowner" squadron into VFC-111, operating the F-5N in the adversary role. In this way, VFC-13 was able to specialize in the SFARP training and VFC-111 could focus on the FRS training. FRS training differs from SFARP training since the FRS pilots are either just completing or in the process of completing their pilot training prior to be integrated in an actual strike fighter squadron. The location at NAS Key West provides the possibility to conduct supersonic missions over the water but limits the training presentation possibilities since there are no mountains to hide behind.

"Fighting Saints" History

VFC-13 has a proud and rich tradition in the history of Naval Aviation and fleet support. The squadron formed in 1973 as VC-13 and was equipped with F-8H Crusaders and developed into the present adversary squadron operating the former ex-Swiss Air Force F-5N Tiger II. The "Saints" have exemplified pride, professionalism, and safety in all endeavors.

VC-13 was formed on September 1, 1973, at NAS New Orleans, during a reorganization of the Naval Reserve. Initially, the squadron operated the F-8H Crusader, all former members of VSF-76 and VSF-86. In April 1974, the "Saints" transitioned to the single-seat A-4L Skyhawk. As the demand for West Coast fleet support missions increased, the squadron moved to NAS Miramar, California, in February 1976 and transitioned to the more reliable two-seat TA-4J. During 1983, single-seat aircraft returned to VC-13 with the arrival of the A-4E.

VC-13 was proudly redesignated as Fighter Squadron Composite 13 (VFC-13) on April 22, 1988, in recognition of the squadron's evolving mission. At that time, the "Saints" logo was redesigned to reflect the more focused role of fleet adversary support. The new logo displayed the wings worn by the highest classification of the former Soviet Union fighter pilot, the "Sniper." In 1988, the "Saints" transitioned to the A-4F Super Fox, a more powerful and capable version of the Skyhawk and, in October 1993, VFC-13 transitioned to the single-seat, twin-engined F/A-18 Hornet. In 1995, the "Saints" received the 1994 CNO Safety "S," Carrier Air Wing 20 Reserve Golden Wrench award and Noel Davis Trophy (Battle "E"), which earned the squadron the right to proudly display the "S," "M," and "E" on the sides of its aircraft.

Budget cuts associated with post-Cold War "right-sizing" of the Navy resulted in the squadron transitioning to the F-5E/F Tiger II and relocating to NAS Fallon, Nevada, in March 1996. NAS Fallon, the "Saints'" current home, is the primary location for all Navy carrier-based tactical aircrew training. VFC-13 adversary pilots work closely with the NAWDC to provide the best air combat training possible. From 2008 onwards, the F-5E models were replaced by ex-Swiss Air Force acquired F-5N aircraft.

The "Saints" are manned with 43 Navy personnel, including 17 enlisted and 26 officers. The 17 enlisted personnel are a select group of dedicated professionals who provide critical operations, administrative, safety, and training support to the squadron. Maintenance of the squadron's F-5Ns is performed by civilian contractors, employed by Pacific Architects and Engineers. The 26-member officer corps includes 14 Selected Reserve, six Regular Navy, and six Full Time Support officers. These three elements of the "Fighting Saints" team combine to fly over 3,500 adversary sorties per year.

Strike Fighter Advanced Readiness Programs

The Strike Fighter Advanced Readiness Programs are mainly conducted at NAS Fallon. Every carrier air wing will pass through NAS Fallon during its workup period. During a three-week deployment of the carrier air wing at NAS Fallon, the aircrews were submitted to an intensive training that enables the Strike Fighter Wing aircrews to improve their fighting skills against a realistic and creditable adversary component prior deployment on their next cruise. During this three-week training, VFC-13 closely cooperated with the adversary assets appointed to NAWDC.

The "Fighting Saints" provided a formidable dissimilar adversary threat presentation. In order to prepare the fleet carrier air wings, the Navy used the adversary squadrons to replicate the threats squadrons might face during a deployment. The area surrounding NAS Fallon was extremely suitable for this type of training, since it comprised an area of approximately 70 x 150 miles that was indicated as a no-fly zone for commercial aircraft and was the ideal location for adversary training. The range included several bombing practice ranges that enabled the participants to practice any scenario in real time. This area encompassed certain areas over Lake Tahoe and the Sierra Nevada which presented a very wide variety of landscapes. The surroundings presented ideal scenery for the small and agile F-5s to hide in and provided the carrier air wing an as-real-as-possible scenario. With a minimal specified altitude during the different combat training sorties, at low level the F-5 was able to exploit its agility to the maximum.

The VFC-13 cooperated with the assets from NAWDC, which are mainly F-16s and F/A-18s. Together they acted as "Red Air," operating against the aircraft of the carrier air wings, "Blue Air."

During a typical sortie, the aircraft of the carrier air wing launched and flew to the most northern area of the range. The adversary aircraft launched during or immediately after the aircraft from "Blue Air." Although the aircraft assigned to "Blue Air" were more advanced and had the disposal of an E-2 early warning aircraft, the aircraft from "Red Air" still presented a real-time training partner. The pilots

The single-seat version of the MiG-28 is captured here in June 2017, presenting BuNo 761578 modex AF-13. All 36 low-hour F-5E/F-5F aircraft assigned to VFC-13 are former Swiss Air Force F-5E Tiger II aircraft acquired in 2006, refurbished and modified to an F-5N standard.

of "Red Air" had several big advantages. The first advantage was that the adversary crews knew the terrain and knew where to hide the agile F-5s and F-16s, which was a clear advantage operating at low level, as it makes the aircraft difficult to spot. By knowing the terrain, communicating their location using landmarks and nicknames made situational awareness easier as well. Secondly, the adversary aircraft operating at low level were all painted in a terrain-suitable camouflage. The aircraft operating at high altitude were painted in a multi-tone blue camouflage. The aircraft appointed to "Blue Air" operated their specific mission, fighting their way through the "Red Air" assets.

During the three-week deployment of a carrier air wing, the daily missions developed with an increased difficulty level. With the air wing workup deployment at full swing, sorties could last up to three hours; this presented "Blue Air" with several real-time threats, both on the way in and out, in which the air wing was presented with both low- and high-level attacks, including early warning and electronic warfare capabilities. Prior to every sortie, a pre-flight briefing was provided by a representative of the adversaries to the "Blue Air" squadrons, allowing them to prepare as well as possible. After the sortie, the entire mission was briefed, providing the aircrews of "Blue Air" to evaluate and improve their skills.

Red Training Blue

Every carrier air wing designated as "Blue Air" used its own tactics. The tactics used during a daily mission were all pre-planned and briefed to explain what was going to happen and how the aircrews of "Blue Air" should react when the event occurred. LT Matthew Gottschalk commented: "All participants of both 'Blue Air' and 'Red Air' joining the daily mission use the same frequencies, meaning we're all briefed on what's going to happen during that specific sortie, in order to provide and meet the appropriate training objectives by presenting realistic situations. Diverting from those tactics might degrade the training program. The adversary squadron can decide on how to step up the difficulty level of the training program as they proceed in accordance with the requirements of the 'Blue Air' squadrons."

Usually, when a carrier air wing arrived, they started with a "prowl, walk, run" mentality, which was not very difficult and got the aircrews familiarized with the territory and the basic rules of engagement. As the carrier air wing proceeded through its three-week training, the difficulty level ramped up and developed to the point where it could handle a large variety of situations that might occur during actual air combat missions. Since the pilots in the squadron vary from experienced pilots to newcomers, this familiarization phase allowed these fresher aircrews to pick up the pass at an easier level. By using the assets of NAWDC, such as E-2 early warning capabilities and EA-18 Growler capabilities, "Red Air" increased the difficulty level for "Blue Air," where it was confronted with "jamming" and situations in which adversaries were hung up behind mountains or flew beneath them.

The Navy is expected to buy an additional 22 aging fighter jets from Switzerland. Navy representatives and armasuisse, the Swiss defense procurement agency, discussed the deal in July 2020. The sole source contract is expected to be finalized in the second quarter of FY2021.

Initially, these training missions took place during daytime but, as the program proceeded, the same scenarios were trained during nighttime missions. Since VFC-13 did not operate using night-vision goggles, the low-level training missions were exclusively conducted during daytime mission.

LT Matthew Gottschalk further explained, "Although there are occasions where 'Red Air' defeats 'Blue Air', winning is not the goal of the adversary squadron. On one hand, it is a great accomplishment since it proves that 'Red Air' is challenging the 'Blue Air' participants so as not to give them an easy ride. The main purpose of 'Red Air' is always to test the 'Blue Air' and try to determine what was performed well and what was performed incorrectly. Whether it is an issue with the radar mechanics, the ability, lack of situational awareness, or any other cause, the result has to be clarified and evaluated after the mission in order to improve future sorties. Although it is not gratifying to win, 'Red Air' participants, however, pull all stops in order to train the 'Blue Air' squadrons in order to make them better."

A Typical Day at the Office

Each day during the three-week training course started with a mission coordination briefing. The overall lead briefed "Blue Air" and this was performed daily to ensure everyone was on the same page. This provided information concerning the radio frequencies in use during the daily mission, the used air space, the daily weather conditions, and the daily training rules, which were the specific safety rules. These training rules should not be violated at any time. This part of the briefing was mainly the same during the duration of the three-week training, but it could vary in detail depending on daytime or nighttime missions.

The Swiss Air Force F-5E Tiger IIs were delivered in 1976. Since the level of maintenance was high and the number of operational hours on the airframes was low, the aircraft were very interesting for the Navy to acquire. This aircraft, former Swiss Air Force serial number J-3027, is now assigned to VFC-13, operating as BuNo 761552.

After the completion of each training scenario, an evaluation takes place with "Blue Air" teams to discuss any improvements that can be implemented in the tactics of the air wing or a specific crew.

Once the coordination briefing was completed, the overall lead asked "Blue Air" the preferences of the aircrews to generate a plan that will fulfill the specific training requirement demands. The overall lead then returned to "Red Air" and determined the plan to be executed by them during that specific mission.

Upon completion of the briefing, all assets took off at specific times to perform their specified sorties. Although an average mission took approximately 20 minutes, the entire sortie took roughly an hour to get the jets airborne and in the correct position. During the flight, information was gathered and collected, and all shots were recorded. Upon completion of the mission, all participants were de-conflicted prior to their return to base.

Upon return at their home base, "Red Air" participants were debriefed by means of an overall debrief, where all the information and experiences during that mission were discussed. During this evaluation, "Red Air" assessed the information and attended a mass debrief with "Blue Air," which was coordinated by the latter. During that debrief, a display presented all available information, recordings, and movies of the mission in order to evaluate that specific mission. Representatives of "Red Air" were present during this debrief to answer any questions or comments "Blue Air" might raise on situations that occurred and follow up on any shots that were taken, mission discrepancies, or training rule violations; it was meant to keep everybody on the same page concerning the completed mission, and to evaluate if the training objectives were met. This entire evolution could take up to seven hours, even though the actual fight could be limited to only 20 minutes.

The available time of a specific mission could last anywhere between 20 minutes and three hours. However, the fuel load of an F-5 was sufficient to keep the aircraft within that area from 20 minutes up to an hour, depending on the fuel consumption required for the sortie and on the application of the afterburner. As such, with some of the training events lasting three hours, "Red Air" launched several waves into the area of operation and rotated jets in and out to present one complete scenario.

Since VFC-13 performed the role of "the bandits," it was its overall responsibility to ensure that this all happened expeditiously and in a safe manner; as this was its role every day, it was the keeper of the safety rules.

Keeping Up with Developments

In a continuously changing world, with developing technology, the tactics used by possible future adversaries develop as well. This means that the adversary squadrons are continuously studying to "keep up" with the latest developments and adapt their "Red Air" tactics. With the arrival of the next-generation fighters, it is difficult to keep up since the assets of VFC-13 do not have the required capabilities. Since the F-5N aircraft in the inventory of the "Fighting Saints" has its limitations, it means that, if it has to go up against the latest generation fighters, the squadron is unable to replicate that situation since the

The F-5 is a very agile aircraft and, although it does not possess the latest generation technology, the aircraft is very maneuverable and extremely suitable as an adversary.

In an equal manner, the aircraft from VFC-13 gather in their designated area prior to the projected scenario during either the pre-deployment training or the Top Gun mission of the day. During the pre-deployment training, large force exercises, all available assets are "thrown" at the air wing, confronting them with all aspects of adversary capabilities.

performance and capabilities on avionics are limited on offensive or defensive systems. The pilots are very experienced and know how to exploit the F-5 to the maximum and bring this to the fight, but you cannot take an F-5 and replicate the F-35 in the same way. The squadron has been operating the F-5 for a long time and has proved it to be a suitable platform, but recent technological developments might be a reason to replace the F-5 with a type of aircraft that is able to replicate these developed performance and capabilities. The US Air Force has replaced the F-5s in the past for more modern F-16 and F-15 fighters, in order to adapt. By 2020, the Navy started to integrate the Super Hornets into the adversary role as well to replicate realistic scenarios during training. A further upgrade to the F-16 is also desired. The F-16 has an increased on-station time of fuel that allows the squadron to stay in the actual training zone for an extended time. Besides that, the F-16 is hard to see and exceptionally fast. There are F-16s from NAWDC present at NAS Fallon, and aircrews from VFC-13 are qualified to operate the F-16 and occasionally use the F-16 to perform their missions. The US Navy recognized the need for a future modernization but has not affected this into actual plans for replacements.

Expanding Adversary Assets

A recent publication concerning the US Marine Corps adversary capabilities states the USMC is planning to expand its capabilities and set up F-5 detachments at three other bases, in addition to VMFT-101 "Sharpshooters." In addition to the existing training capabilities, the USMC master aviation plan calls for adding light-attack turboprop aircraft to its tactical training fleet, such as the AT-6C Coyote or A-29 Super Tucano. The USMC F-5 fleet requirements have significantly grown in the past years and the gap is growing increasingly.

External Adversary Capabilities

Currently, a small number of contractors are used to supplement the existing Navy capabilities. These contractors use different aircraft types than the Navy, like the Hawker Hunter, Aero L-39, IAI Kfir, and the Dassault Mirage F1. Since these contractors execute their mission using the same presentation as the Navy adversary squadrons, the sole difference is the pilot and the dissimilar air combat capability of the aircraft used. This enables the CAW aircrews in training to experience something different than an F/A-18 as their opponent.

The number of external contractors is slowly increasing. Currently, there are three external contractors providing their services to the Air Force, Navy, and Marines. These are Draken Air, TacAir, and Airborne Tactical Advantage Company (ATAC). Recently, it was announced that ATAC expanded its capabilities by acquiring a batch of ex-French Air Force Mirage F1 fourth-generation fighters. These aircraft were bought to close the gap between the fifth-generation fighters currently integrated in the operational fighter squadrons and the adversary squadrons. It further stipulated that ATAC currently had a contract to supply a total of 5,000 hours of adversary training. It mentioned that the US Navy demanded a total of 5,000 hours for the next year of adversary training of fourth-generation "Red Force" capability alone. Moreover, the Air Force might even reserve a total of 37,000 hours.

By the end of 2020, the NAVAIR Specialized and Proven Aircraft Program Office PMA-226, Adversary Integrated Product Team issued a notice they will initiate a F-5N/F capability upgrade or block upgrade program modification and overhaul as part of the F-5N+/F+ Avionics Reconfiguration and Tactical Enhancement/Modernization for Inventory Standardization (ARTEMIS) program.

Furthermore, the Naval Air Warfare Center Aircraft Division (NAWC-AD) intends to repatriate 16 F-5E and six F-5F ex-Swiss Air Force Tiger II aircraft. As part of repatriation, these aircraft will require integration of the Block Upgrade Program and all associated prerequisite technical directives.

This notice also included that the government intends to award a contract to Tactical Air Support, Inc in the second quarter of FY2021 to acquire additional adversary capability. NAWC-AD also intends to award a contract to Tactical Air Support, Inc for a five-year ordering period from March 15, 2021 until March 14, 2026.

"Red Air" launches several adversary waves during a large force exercise. The "Blue Air" wing is presented with several real-time scenarios during one sortie.

Chapter 18

Remaining Developments

This section will cover the improvements that have been made in the remaining fields of Naval Aviation. The modification of the main transport fleet and the modernization of aerial refueling is a specific field that has seen significant progress the past decade and deserves to be investigated further.

Greyhounds for Ospreys

The C-2 Greyhound had a long and respectable service within the US Navy since its introduction in 1966. The successor of the C-2A Greyhound, the CMV-22B Osprey, was announced in 2015. Initial integration of the CMV-22B in the VRC squadrons commenced in 2018, when the Navy purchased the first four CMV-22B aircraft in FY2018 and continued purchasing four CMVV-22Bs per year until FY2020.

In February 2020, the first CMV-22B was completed and delivered to the Navy. A second Osprey arrived at NAS Patuxent River the week before the final round of testing. The fleet of Navy Ospreys should be operational within six years from contract to delivery, carrying out a much wider array of roles than the old Greyhounds executed. They will be flying VIPs and crew back and forth, as do the venerable CODs, but they will also do search and rescue and support for Naval Special Warfare.

The aircraft differs from the Marine Corps and Air Force versions, boasting an enhanced fuel capacity which required wing modifications to deal with the greater weight. There is another key aspect: the CMV-22B, unlike the C-2A, can carry an F-35C engine onboard a carrier.

By November 2020, the Navy had completed its first carrier landings and take-offs of its new CMV-22B Carrier Onboard Delivery (COD) variant successfully. A CMV-22B from Fleet Logistics Multi-Mission Squadron 30 (VRM-30) recovered to the flight deck of the Nimitz-class nuclear-powered aircraft carrier CVN-70 USS *Carl Vinson* for the first time on November 20, 2020. A second CMV-22B operated onto CVN-70 USS *Carl Vinson* on November 21, 2020. This aircraft became the first of its type to be refueled on a carrier.

Fleet Logistics Support Squadron 30, or VRC-30, is based at NAS North Island. The squadron, however, has several detachments on temporary deployment. BuNo 162152 is seen here landing at NAF Atsugi in early 2016, assigned to VRC-30 Det 1.

Fleet Logistic Support Developments

In April 2020, the Navy completed a crucial developmental test and evaluation within its Avionics Obsolescence Upgrade (AOU) program, in order to upgrade the avionics of C/KC-130T Hercules logistics support and aerial refueling aircraft.

The Tactical Airlift Program Office completed a remote assessment of the latest build of the C/KC-130T AOU software configuration over the course of two eight-hour days of testing on April 7–8, 2020. The tests took place using the Operational Flight Trainer, located at the Air Logistics Training Center at NAS Fort Worth Joint Reserve Base.

The two feeds were transmitted live to NAVAIR system and test engineers at Air Test and Evaluation Squadron 20 (VX-20) at NAS Patuxent River, Lockheed Martin engineers in Owego, and Naval Air Warfare Center Training Systems Division engineers in North Carolina, providing the participants with a full understanding of the response of the systems.

Accomplishment of the two-day remote assessment was critical for determining if the software fixed a number of high-priority deficiencies that affected certifications required by the Department of Defense and Federal Aviation Administration. The proactive identification of content problems prior to the delivery of the final software in June and flight tests during the summer decreased the risk of program delays down the line. Test completion of the AOU system is expected in fall 2021.

In 2013, VR-55 took delivery of two KC-130T-30 aircraft, capable of flying an enhanced cargo load over the normal C-130T. This further augmented the squadron's logistics capabilities. In 2014, it saw the replacement of its three C-130Ts with USMC KC-130T airframes. VR-55 currently resides at NAS Point Mugu.

VRC-30 resides at NAS North Island and regular maintenance cycles take place at its facilities. BuNo 162147 was noted at NAS North Island in June 2017, just after a serious wash down of all salty components.

Chapter 19

Naval Aviation Modernization: The Future Air Wing

As the *Naval Aviation Vision 2016–2025* eloquently states, "Naval Aviation forces are forward engaged and ready — every day. Expeditionary forces, amphibious forces, nuclear-powered aircraft carriers, air wings, manned and unmanned platforms, rotary and fixed wing aircraft are on station, valued and in increasingly higher demand. No other service or community can deliver the capabilities of Naval Aviation projects." In the defined strategic plan to 2025, delivering readiness is the preeminent focus of the Navy and Marine Corps.

Naval Aviation leadership's approach to maintaining superiority over the maritime domain is outlined in *Naval Aviation Vision*. Readiness is predicated on the execution of three key strategic elements:

- Ensuring wholeness by managing resources available to organize, man, train, and equip Naval Aviation across its full range of missions;
- Sustaining capability superiority by taking an evolutionary approach to improving already fielded platforms and payloads, and integrating enabling technologies into the battlespace;
- Maintaining sufficient capacity – having the right number of units manned, trained, and equipped in the right configuration to meet demand.

The long-term readiness investments described in this section support the Naval Aviation vision and are the tools by which the Navy will deliver decisive combat power at home and abroad. The long-term vision of Naval Aviation recognizes that readiness investments today and, as we move toward 2025, will remain its top commitment.

In FY2021, United States Naval Aviation proposes to acquire 121 additional aircraft of all kinds, down from 163 acquired in FY2020. Naval Aviation is in generally good shape. Inventories have been

VMFA-314 completed its conversion to the F-35C Lighting II in 2019 and completed its training at NAS Lemoore by VFA-125 "Rough Raiders" while borrowing aircraft from VFA-125. BuNo 169601 modex VW-434 was noted at NAS Lemoore in September 2019. Currently VMFA-314 is assigned to Carrier Air Wing 9 to enable VFA-97 "Warhawks" to complete its conversion from the F/A-18E to the F-35C Lightning II.

stable, the average age for most elements is good, and the Navy has been buying enough aircraft to maintain its inventory. The Navy, however, needs to increase aircraft procurement in the future to maintain current inventories, facing ever higher costs to maintain its aircraft inventory and has been slow to field unmanned aerial vehicles.

To ensure the ability to deter and defeat future potential adversaries, the US Naval Aviation will continue to innovate and invest in platforms, payloads, sensors, and communications required to secure access, project power, and enable sea control in the future fight. In doing so, it will focus on making smart investments that support Naval Aviation's ability to deliver required warfighting readiness while preserving the capability and sustainability of the future force.

This evolution is deliberate and will span the full spectrum of Naval Aviation missions and activity. New warfighting capabilities and positive changes will be evident in the significant expansion of the live, virtual, and constructive training capabilities; the fielding of the F-35B/C Lightning II aircraft with its low observable stealth technology and integrated sensor suite; further implementation of the Magic Carpet project to improve pilot proficiency in the carrier landing environment; the quantifiable advances in supply chain management to boost material readiness; the design and commission of the transformational Gerald R. Ford-class carrier; the enterprise's ability to leverage additive manufacturing and digital thread to enable faster maintenance and repairs; the flexibility and growing capability of our unmanned family of systems; the keen focus on innovative ways to train and manage the talent resident in the people of Naval Aviation. These are examples of evolving capability, but they are not all-inclusive.

Naval Aviation will continue to move forward, with transitioning nearly every legacy aircraft to a more technologically advanced platform while maintaining a system-of-systems approach. Naval Aviation will also make certain warfighters are equipped with next-generation weapons and will develop weapons with modular components that can be swapped out and tailored for specific targets.

Naval Aviation is an in-demand force that serves essential, unique roles around the globe, often serving as the first line of defense far from US shores. Naval Aviation will continue to ensure its current and future readiness to respond when the nation calls. Whether operating from sea or land, from aircraft carriers, austere forward deployed locations, or main base facilities, the Naval Aviation forces will be trained, equipped and ready to achieve mission success. Consistent with "Naval Aviation Vision," the developments covered in this book prove its commitment to the three pillars of capability, readiness, and capacity. In uncertain and increasingly contested environments, Naval Aviation will continue to provide a persistent, flexible, forward-deployed force that will remain a stabilizing presence around the world.

The first unmanned rotary MQ-8B drones have been integrated within the Navy. Seen here is BuNo 168446 modex N22 with HSC-23 "Wildcards" at NAS North Island in June 2017.

References

Air Power at Sea: A Century of US Naval Aviation 1911–2011, Navy League of the United States Hampton Roads Council, Virginia (2011)

Naval Aviation Vision 2016–2025, The United States Marine Corps and Department of the Navy, independently published (2016)

https://www.airpac.navy.mil/Organization/
https://www.airpac.navy.mil/Organization/Carrier-Air-Wing-CVW-2/
https://www.airpac.navy.mil/Organization/Carrier-Air-Wing-CVW-5/
https://www.airpac.navy.mil/Organization/Carrier-Air-Wing-CVW-9/
https://www.airpac.navy.mil/Organization/Carrier-Air-Wing-CVW-11/
https://www.airpac.navy.mil/Organization/Carrier-Air-Wing-CVW-17/
https://www.airpac.navy.mil/Organization/Naval-Aviation-Warfighting-Development-Center/About-Us/
https://www.airpac.navy.mil/Organization/Strike-Fighter-Squadron-VFA-86/
https://www.airpac.navy.mil/Organization/Strike-Fighter-Squadron-VFA-97/
http://www.gonavy.jp/CVLocation.html
http://www.scramble.nl
http://www.seaforces.org
http://www.thedrive.com